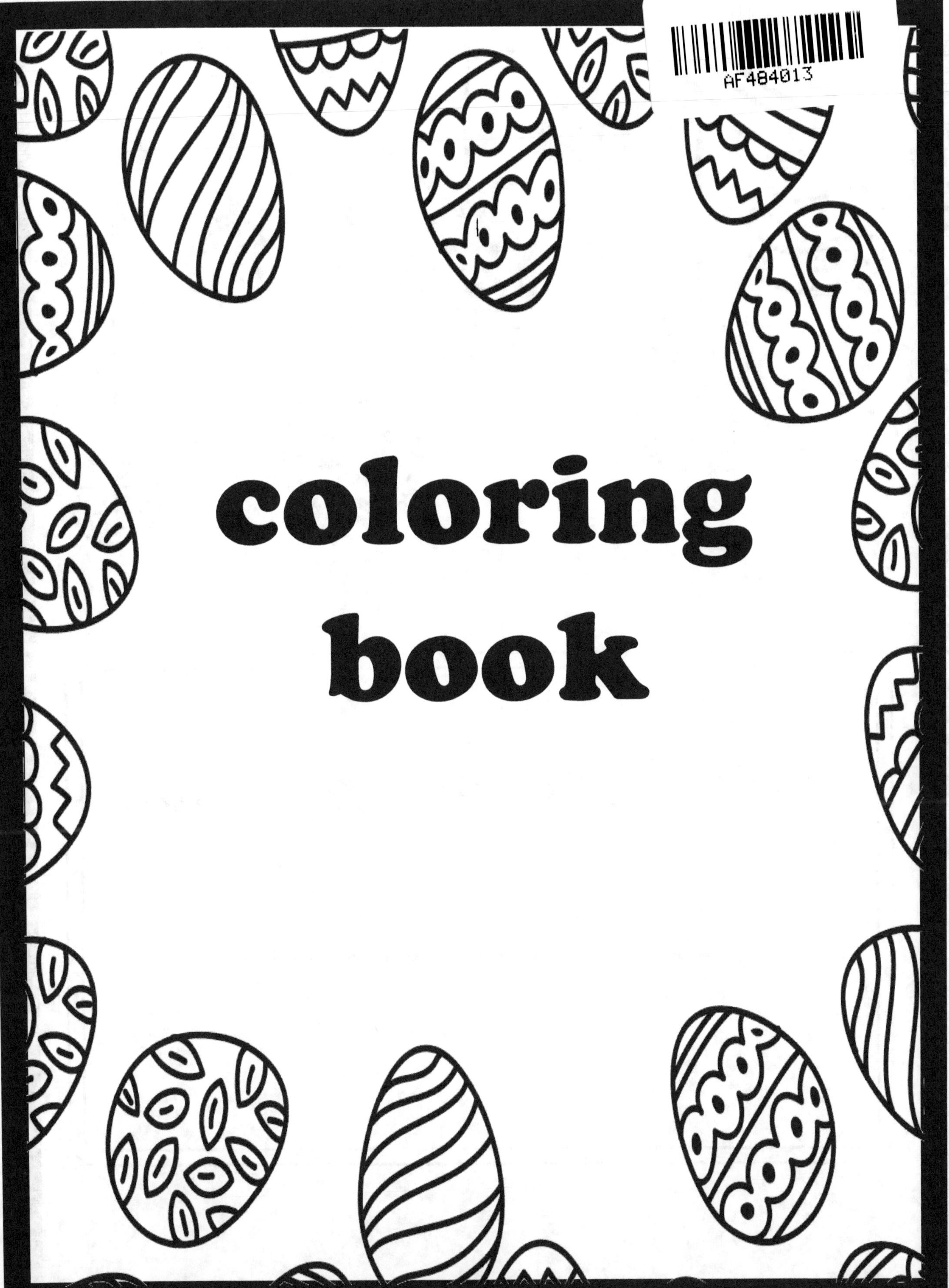

coloring
book

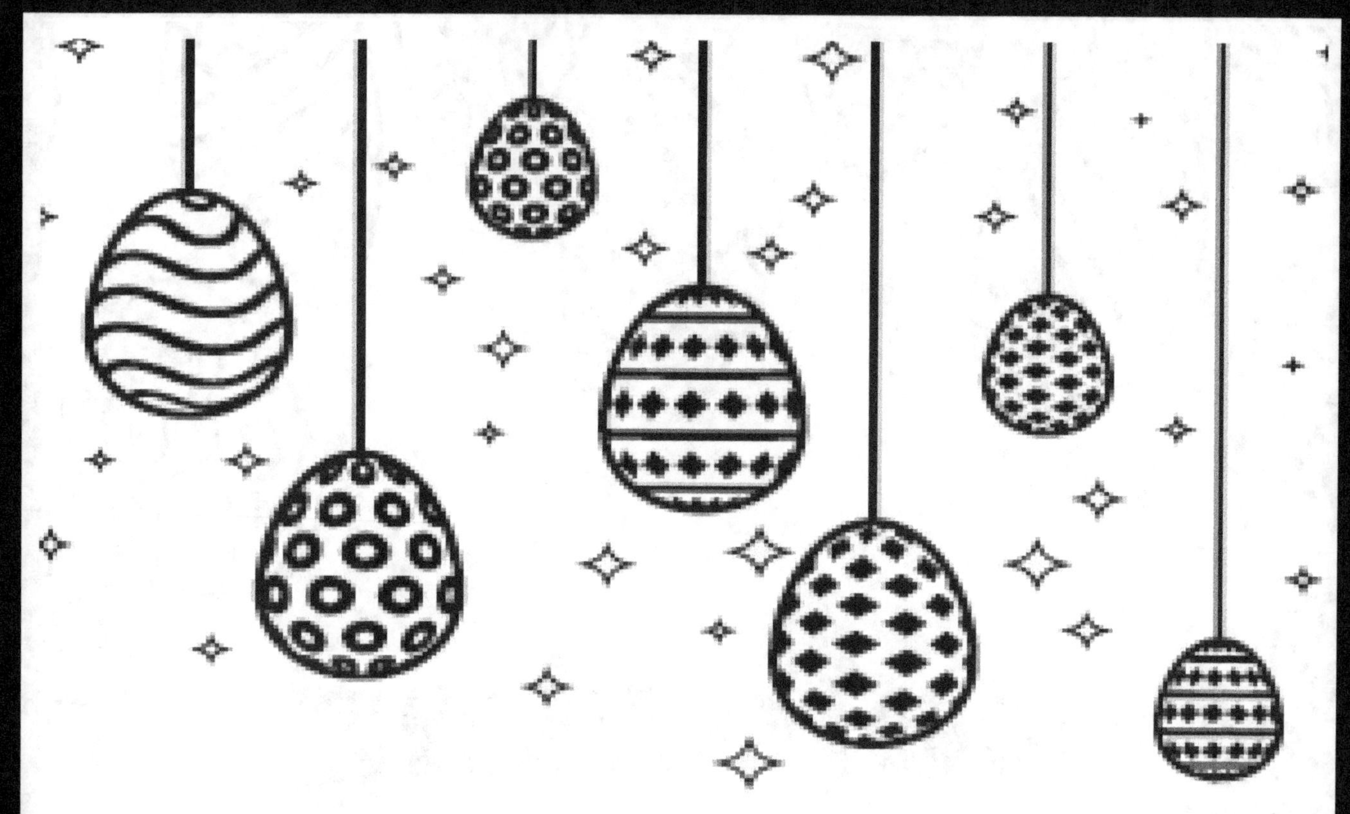

this book belongs to:

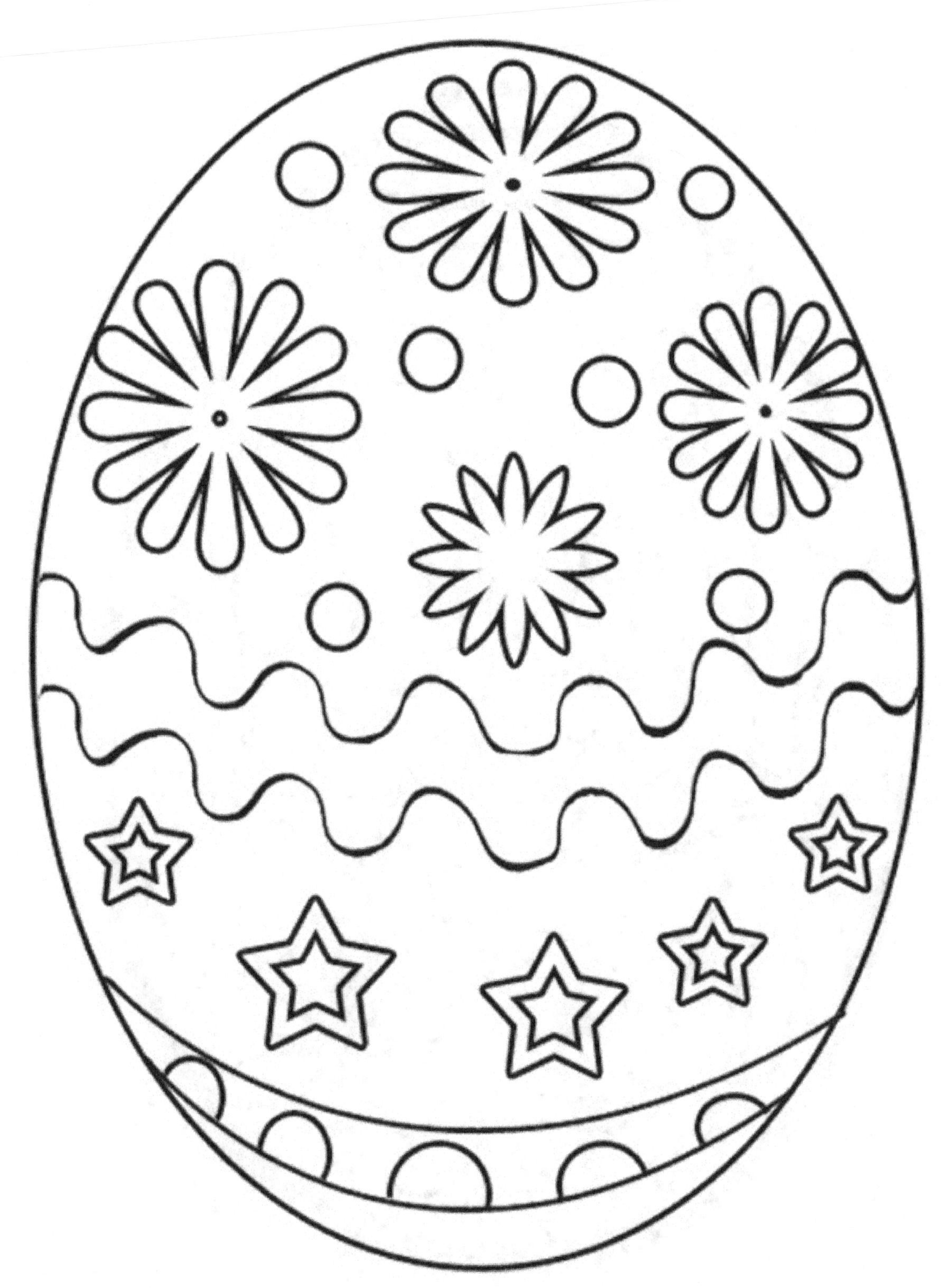

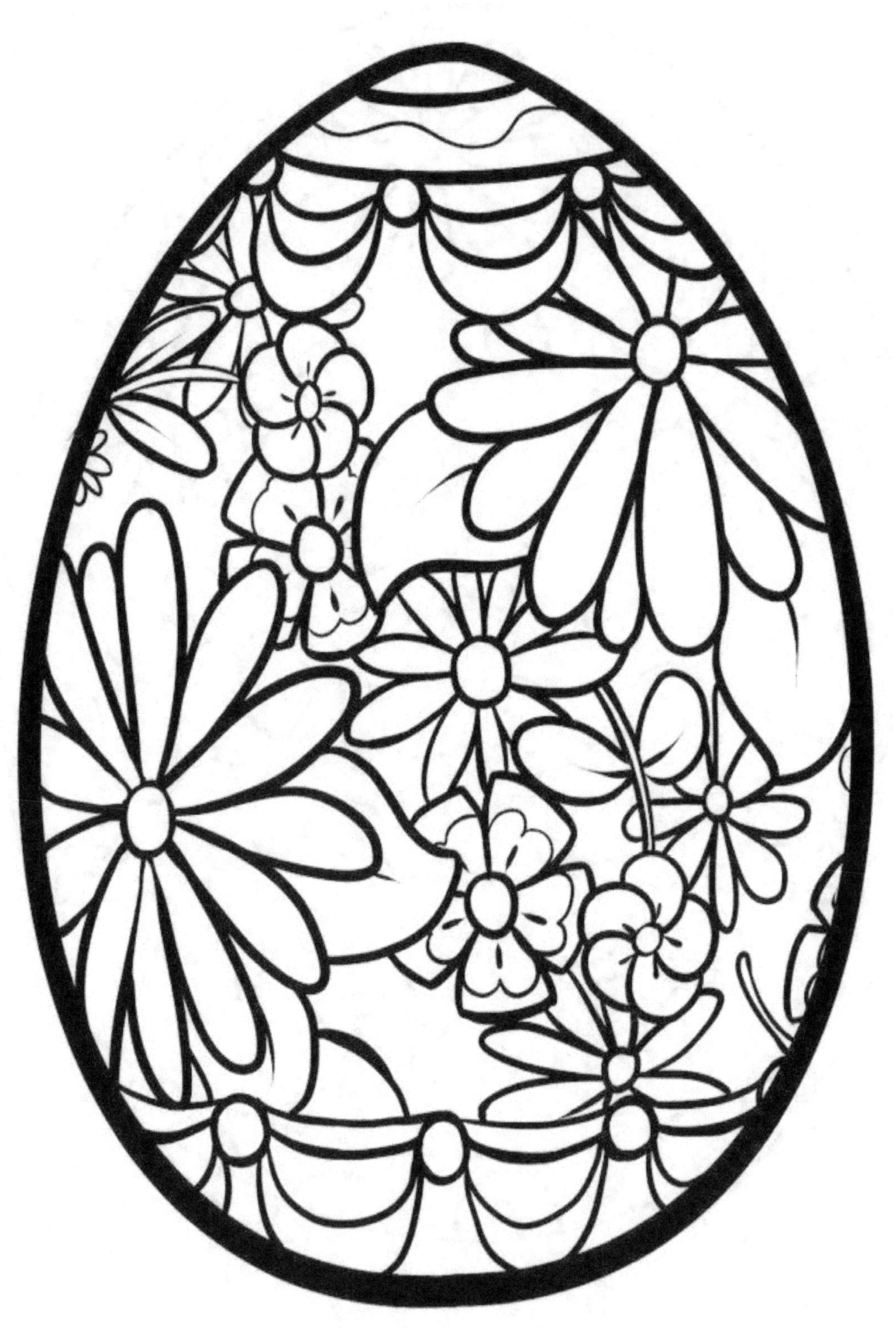

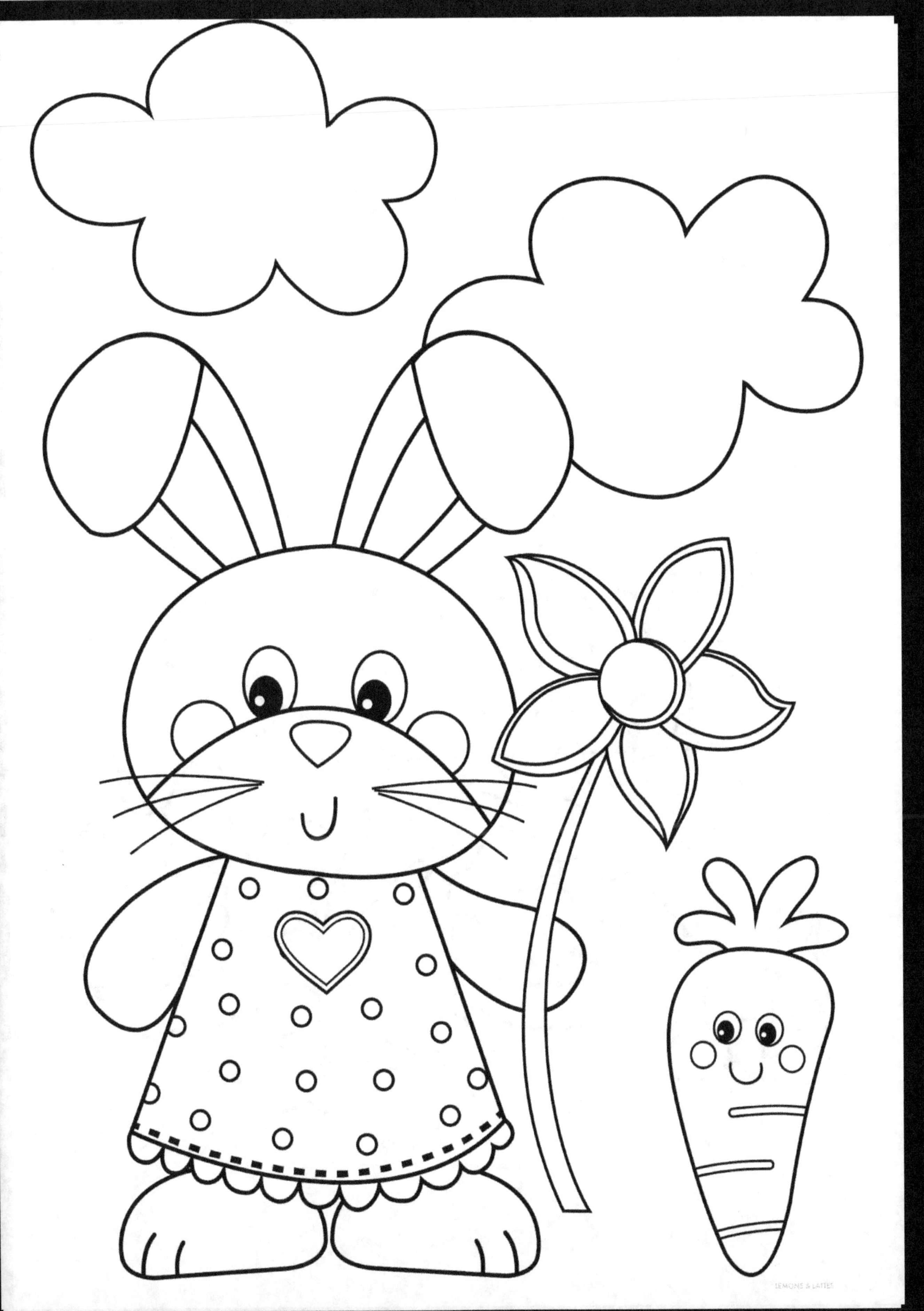

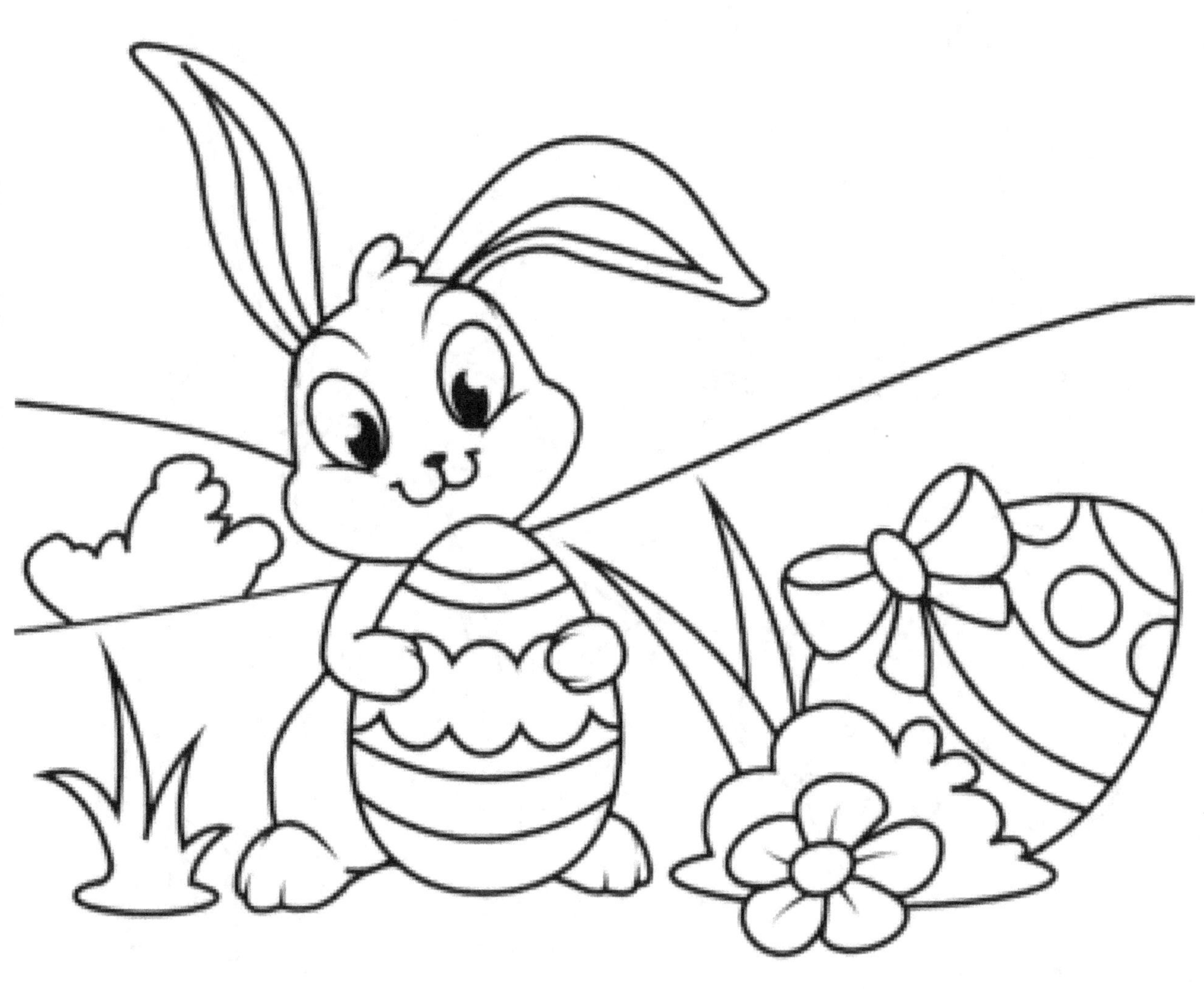

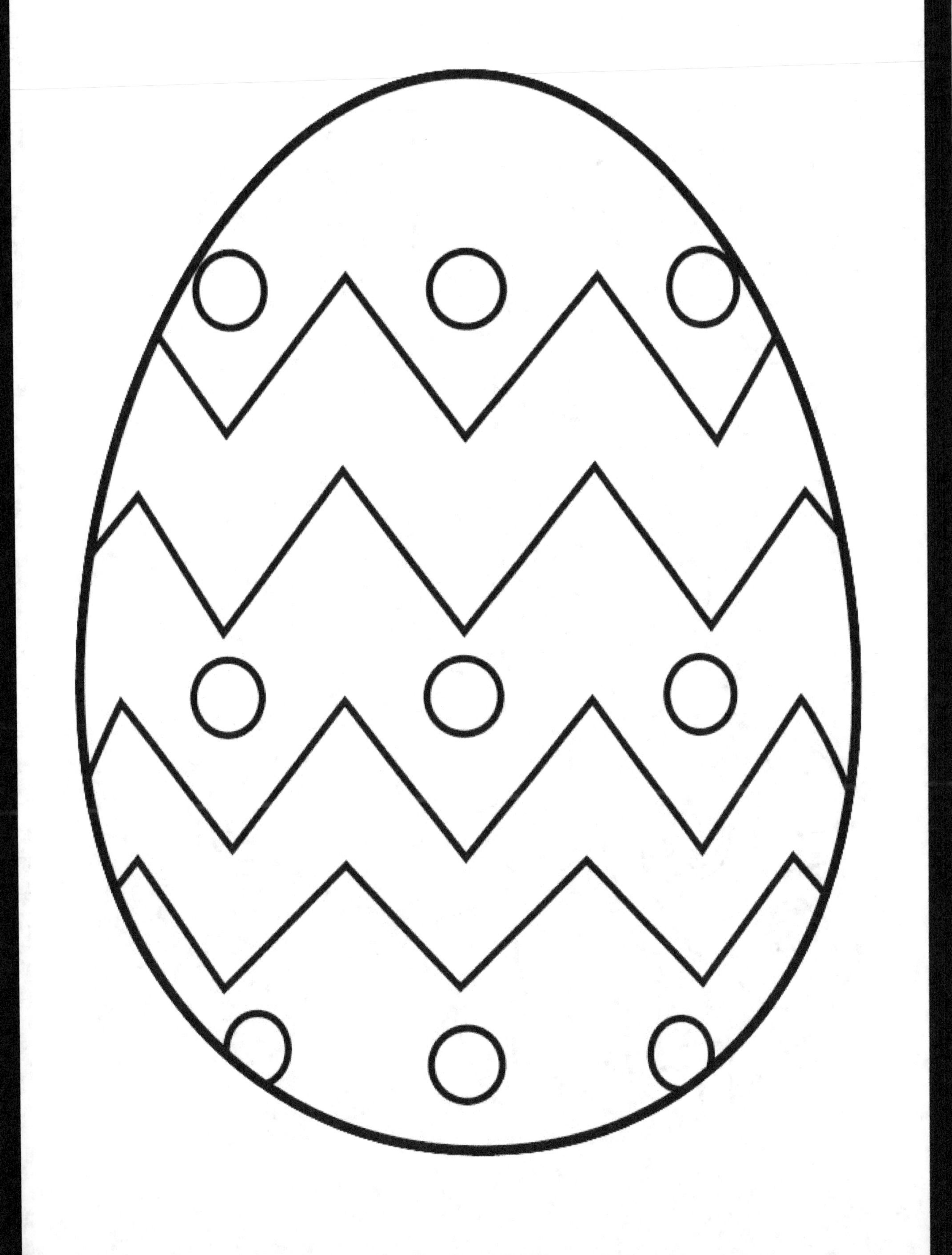

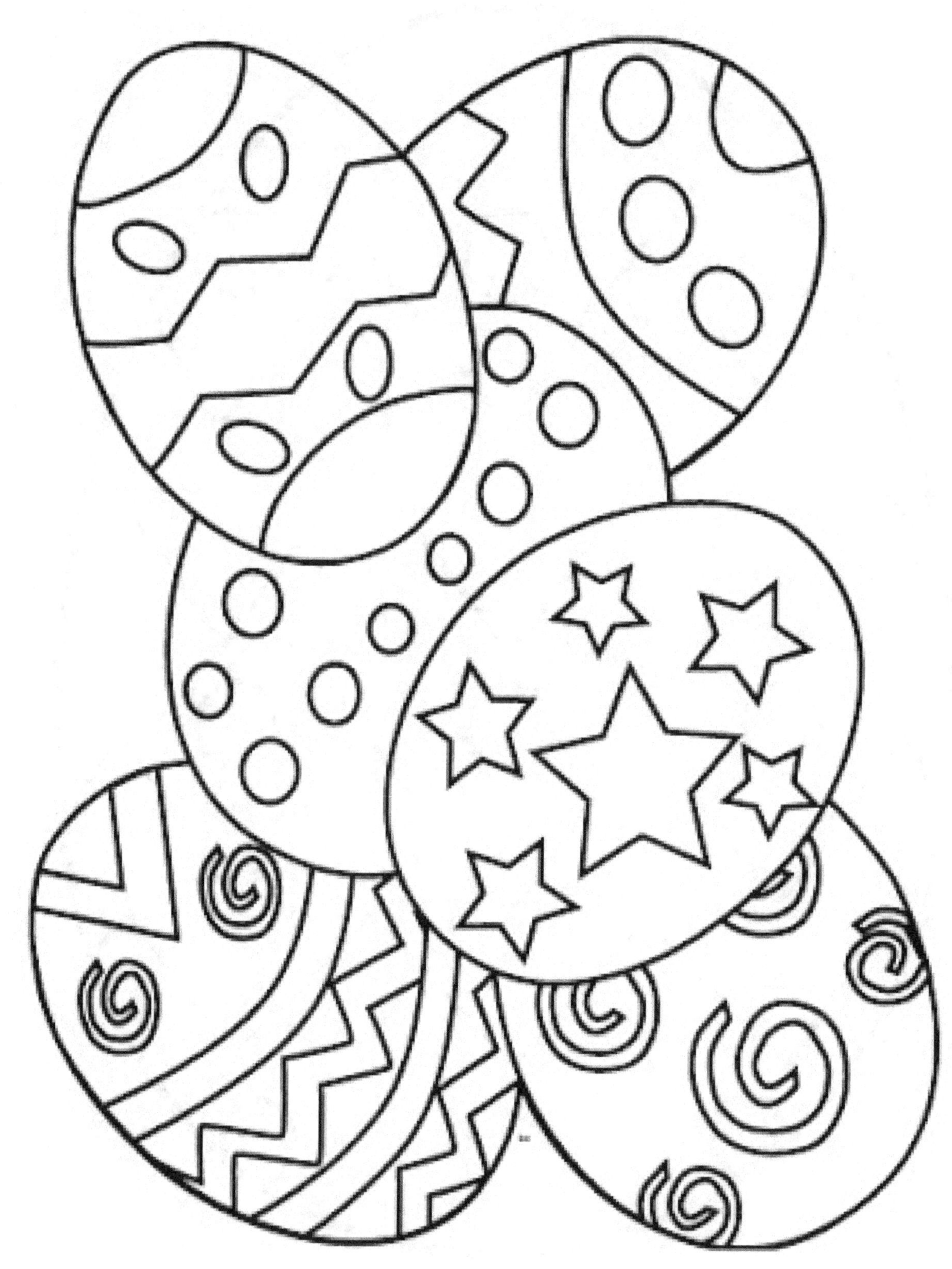

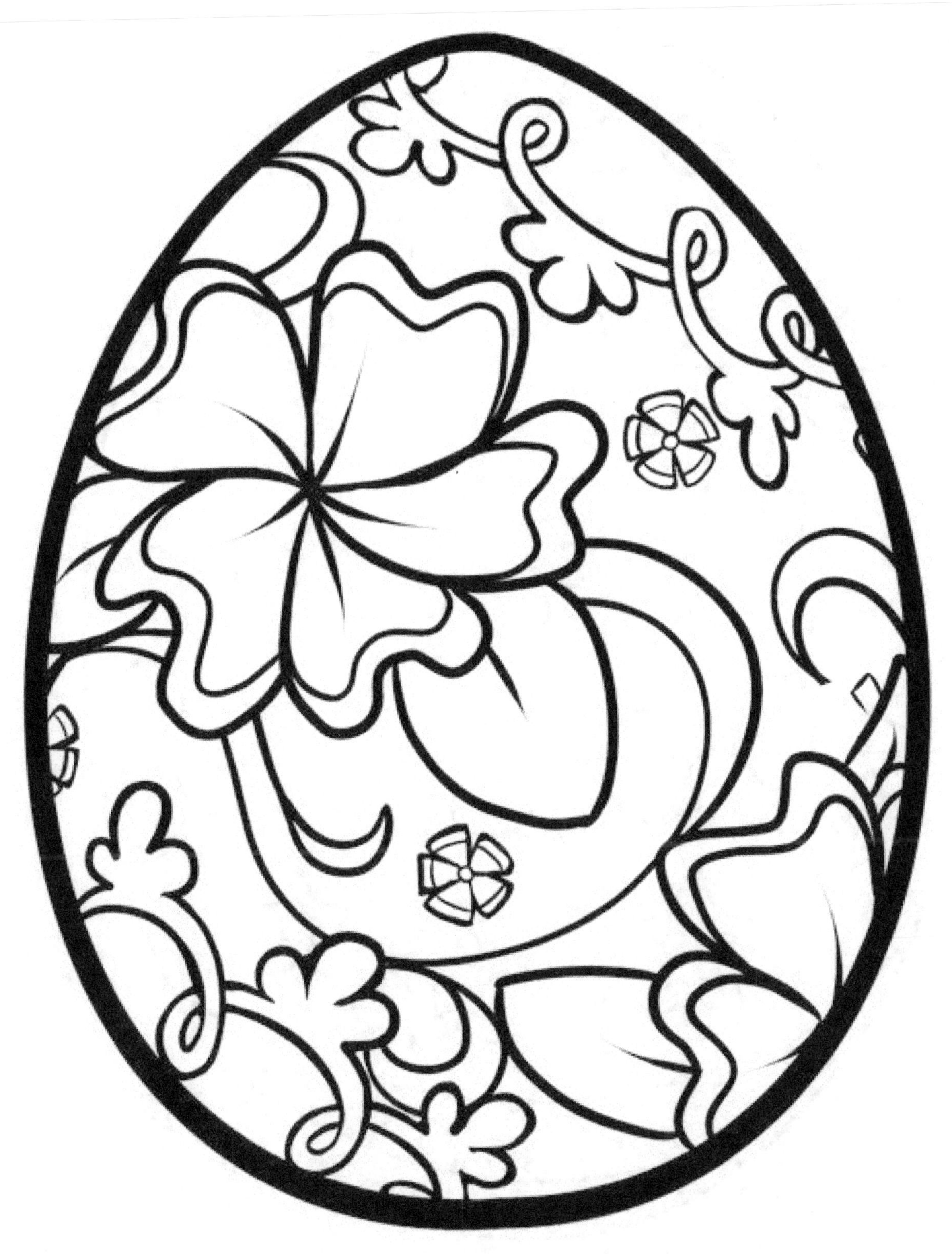

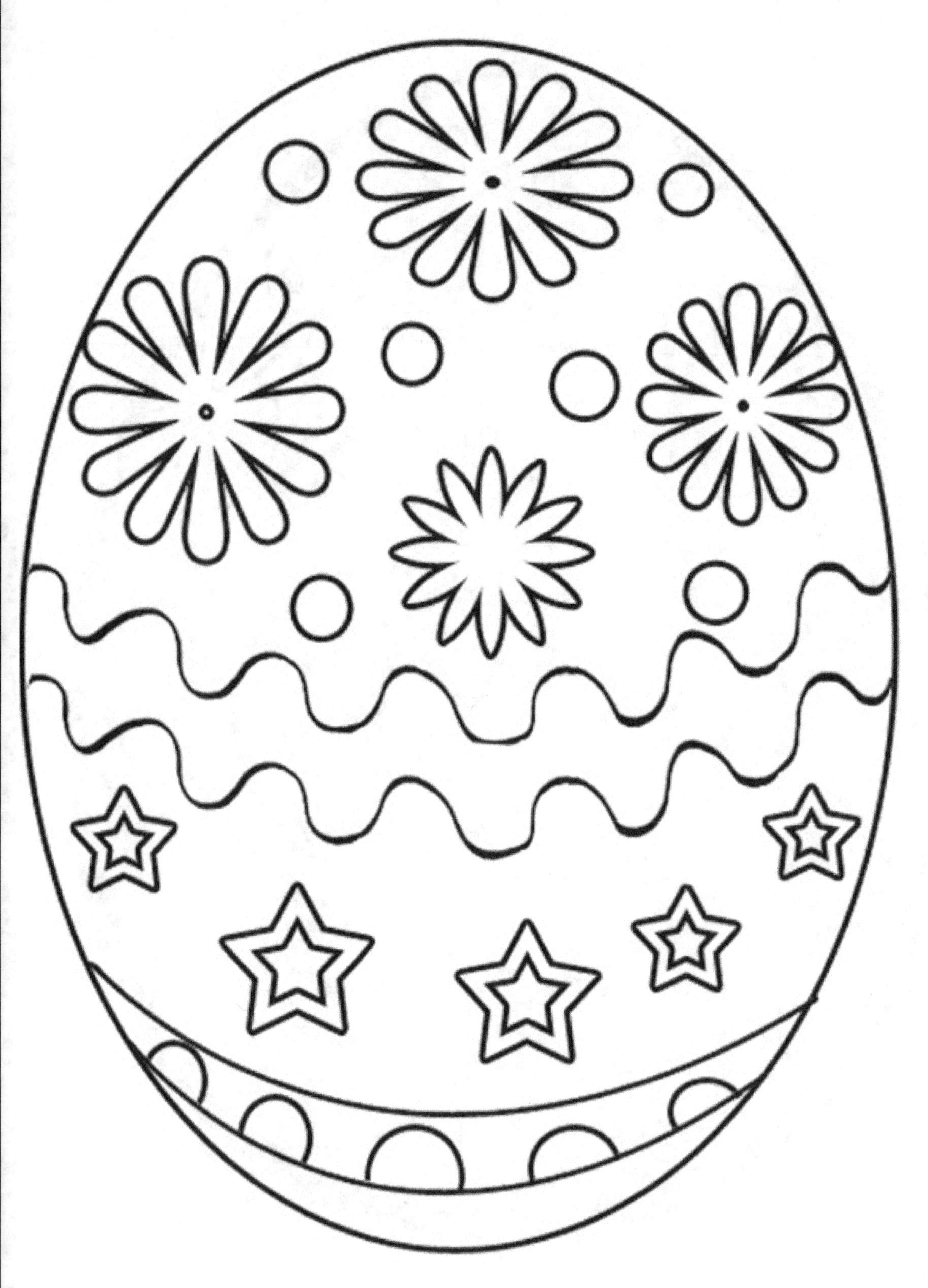

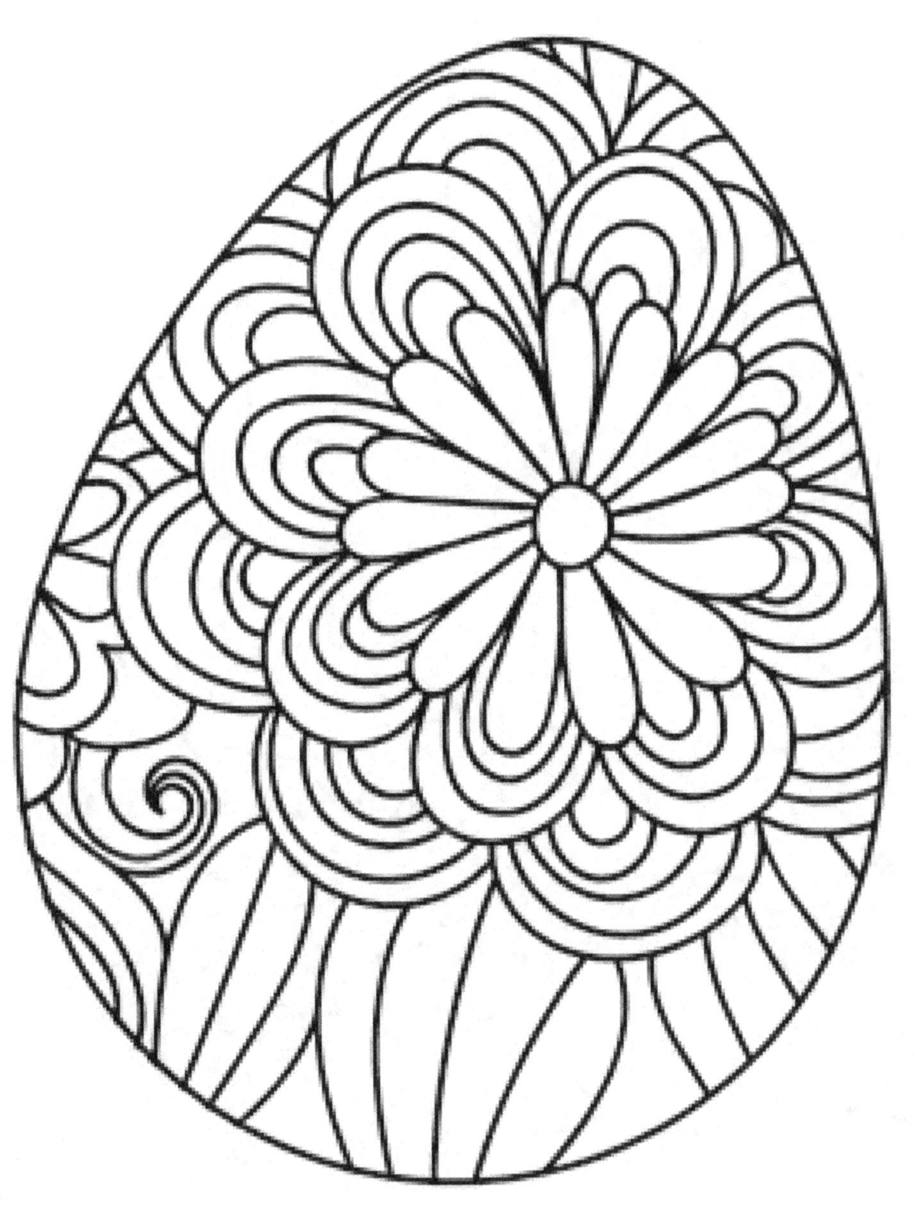

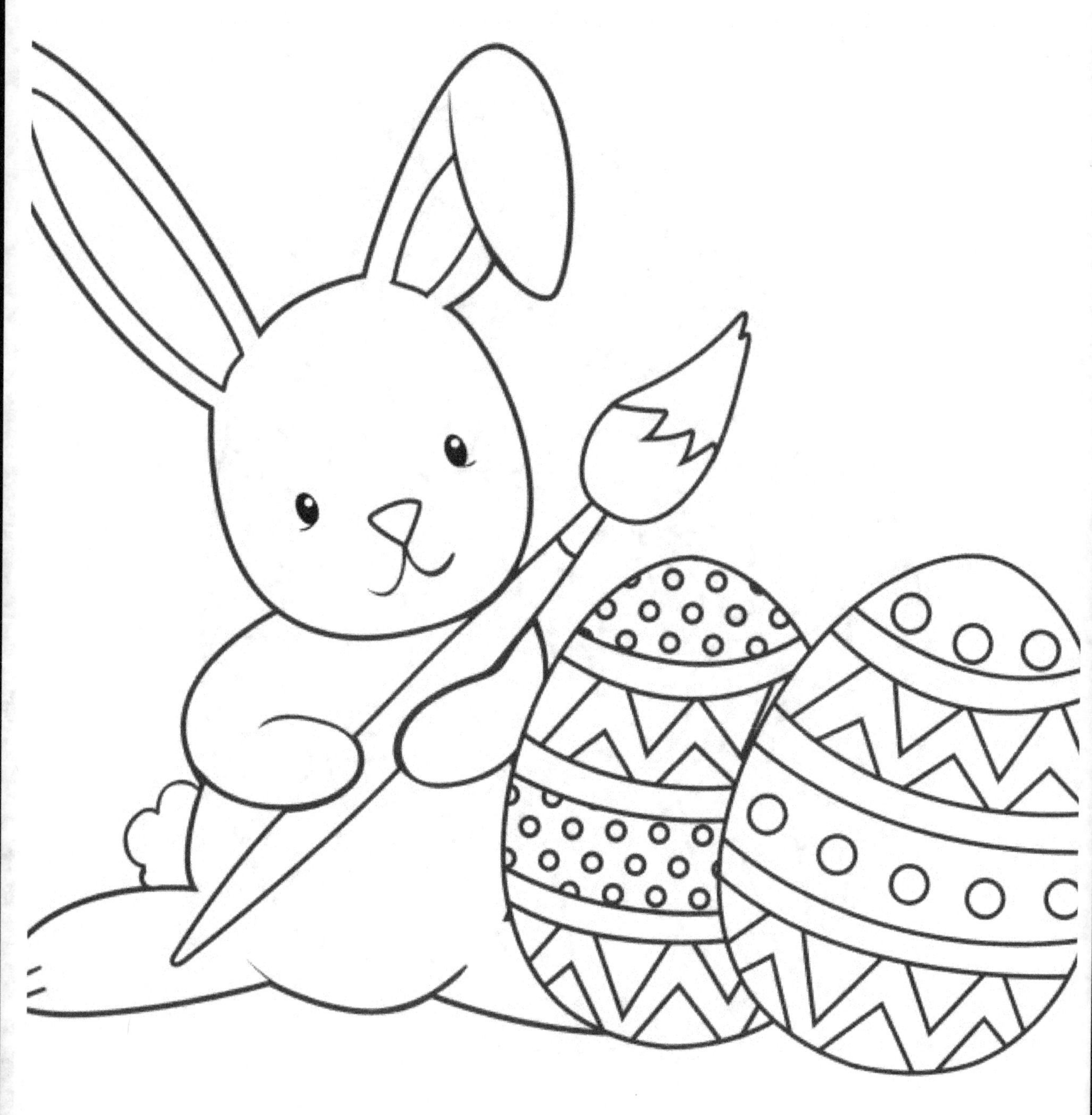

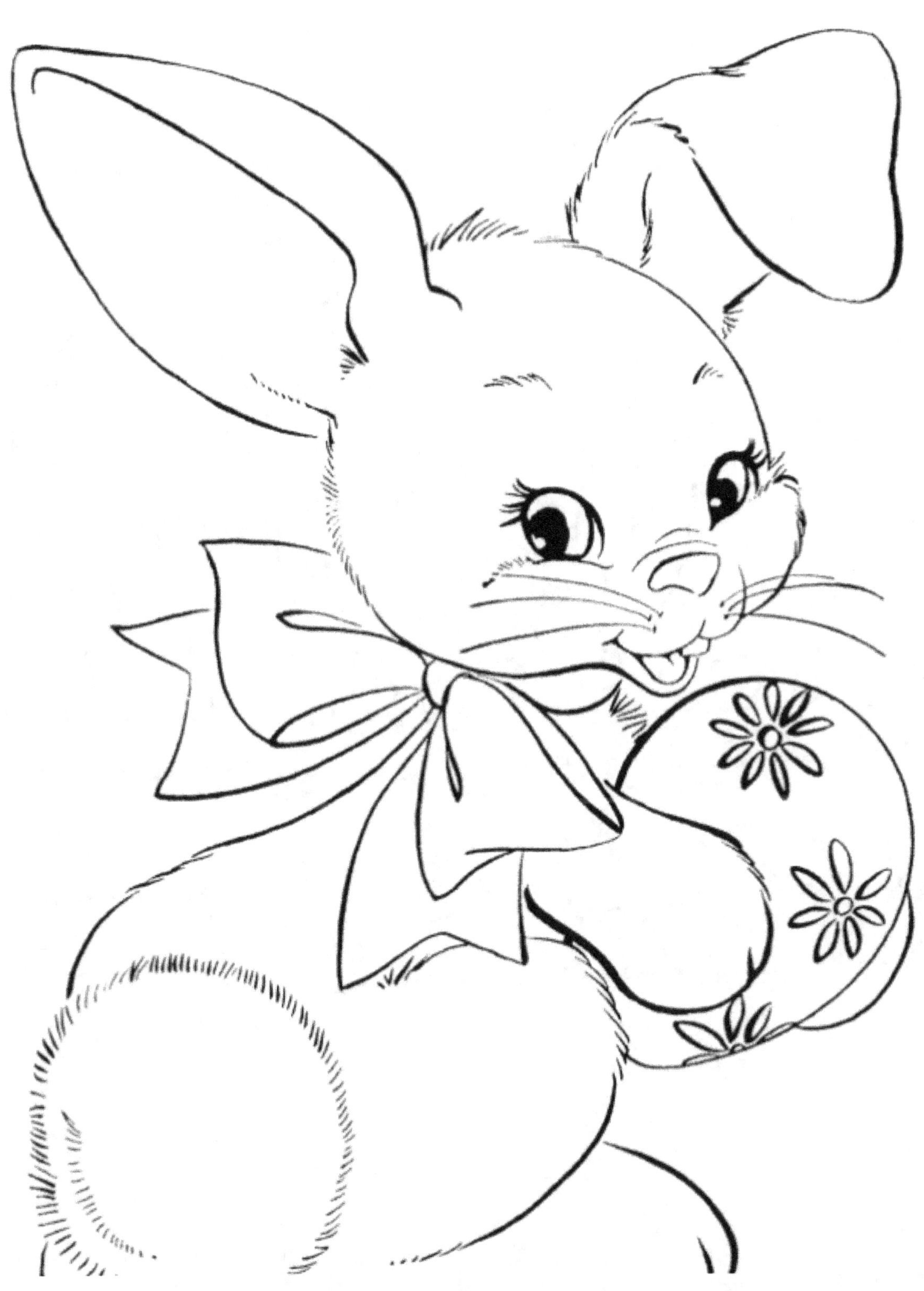

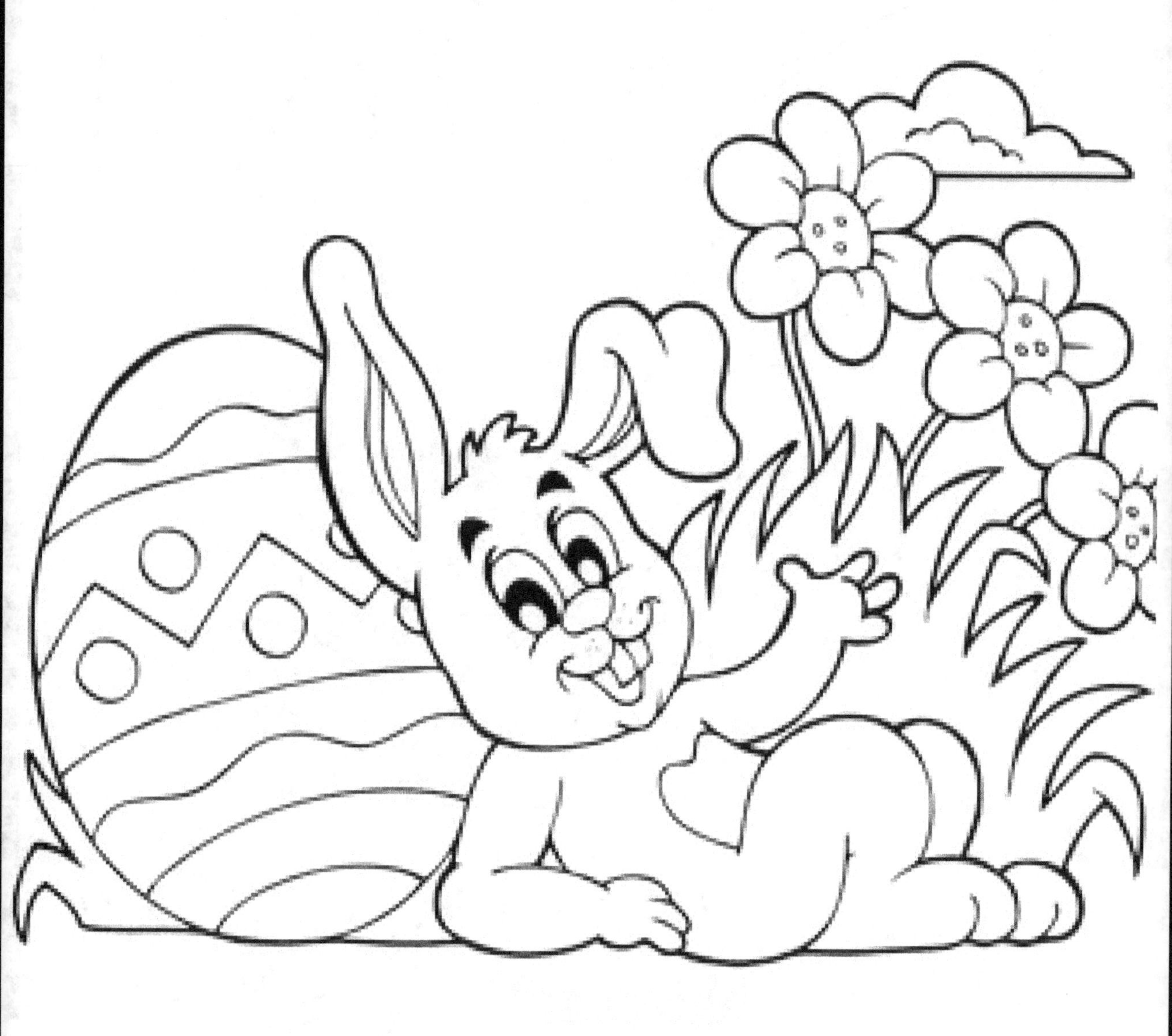

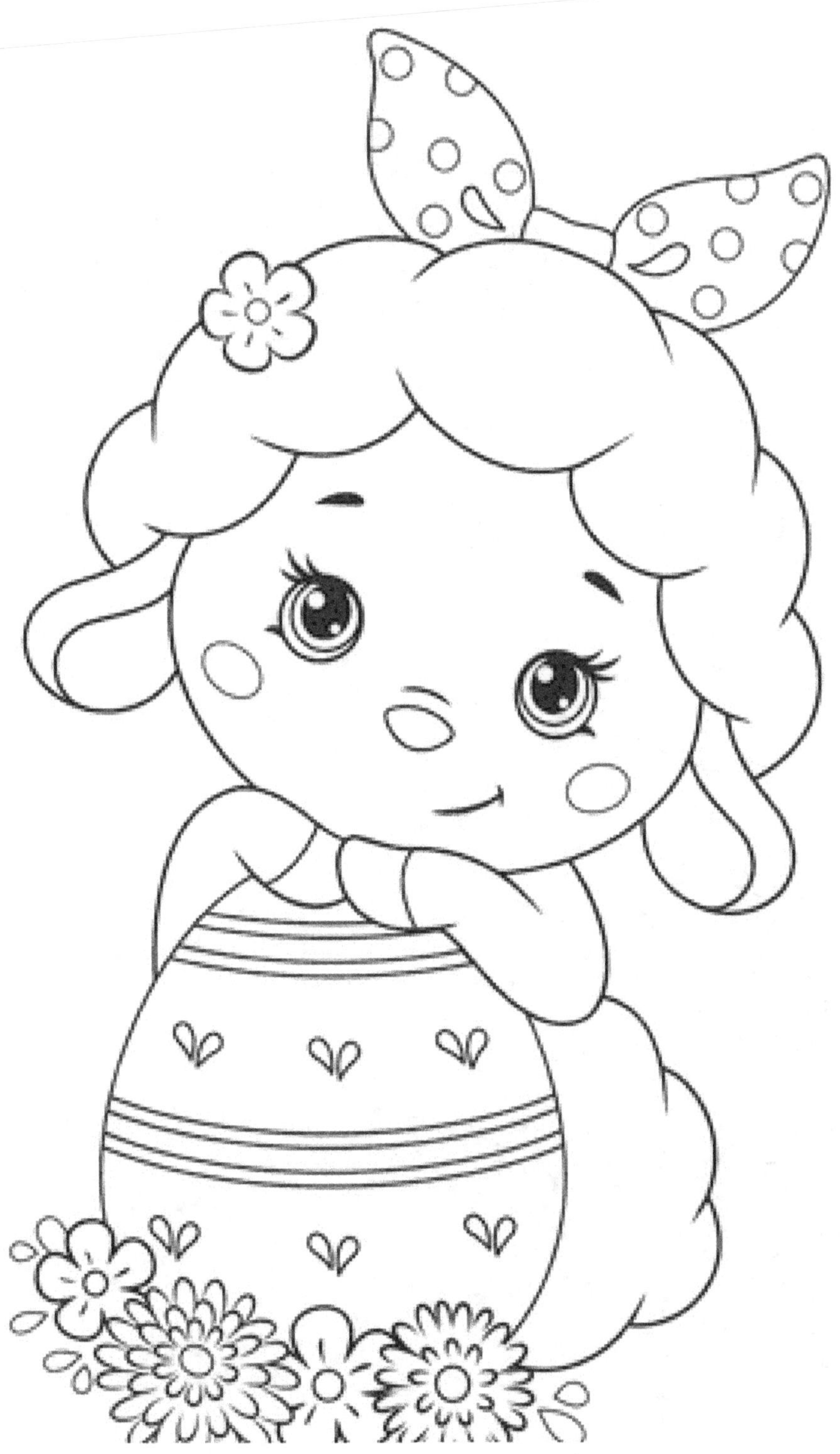

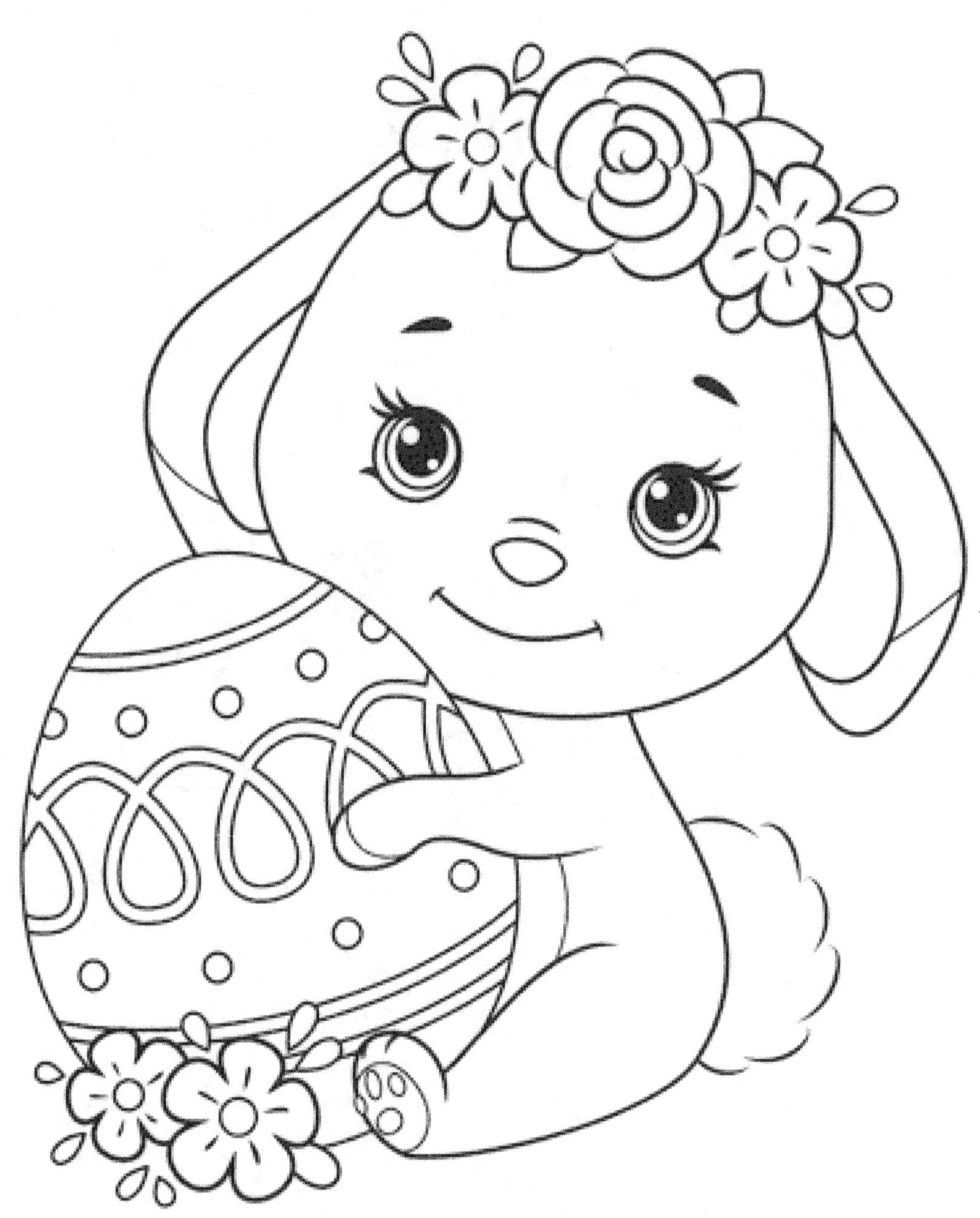

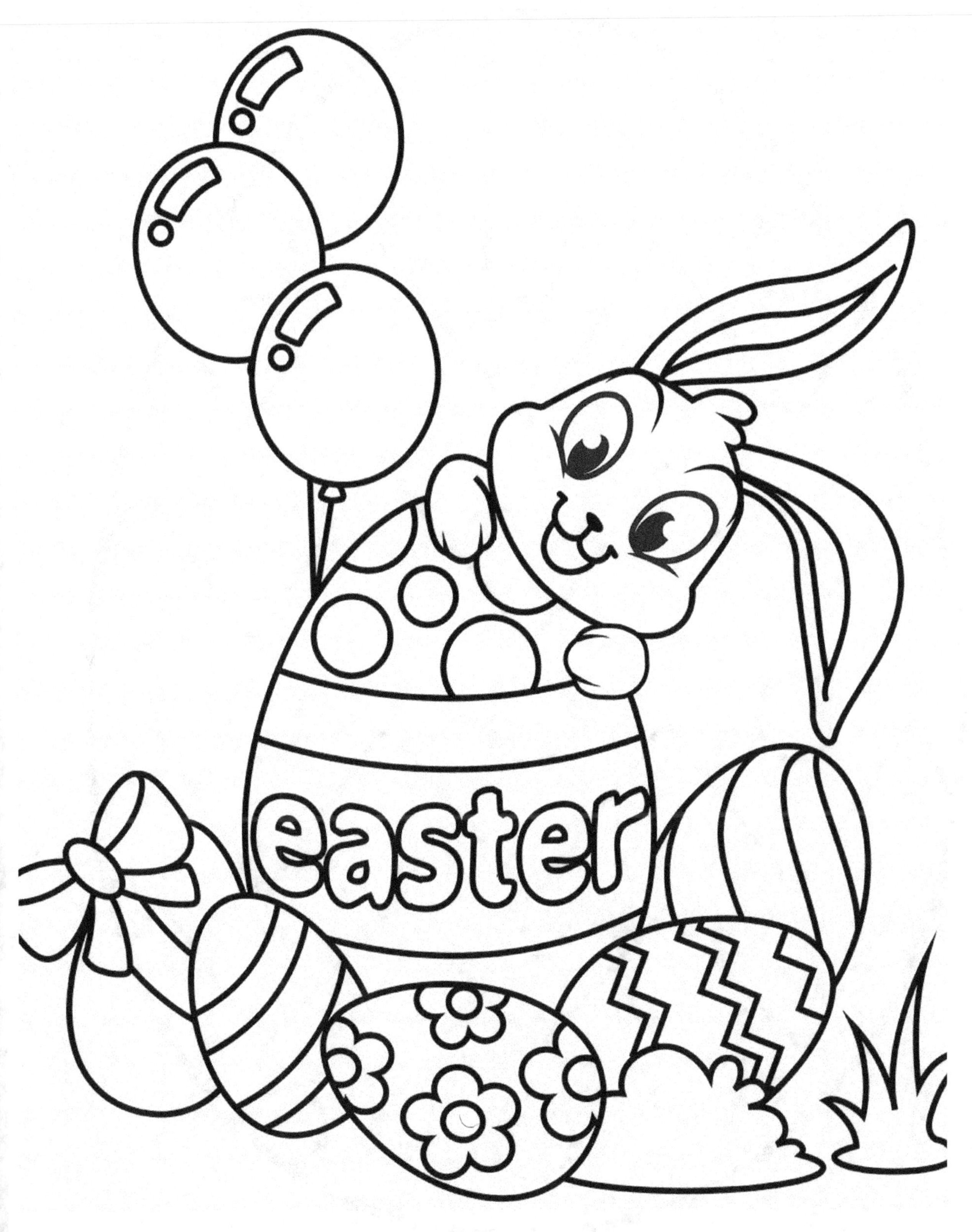
easter

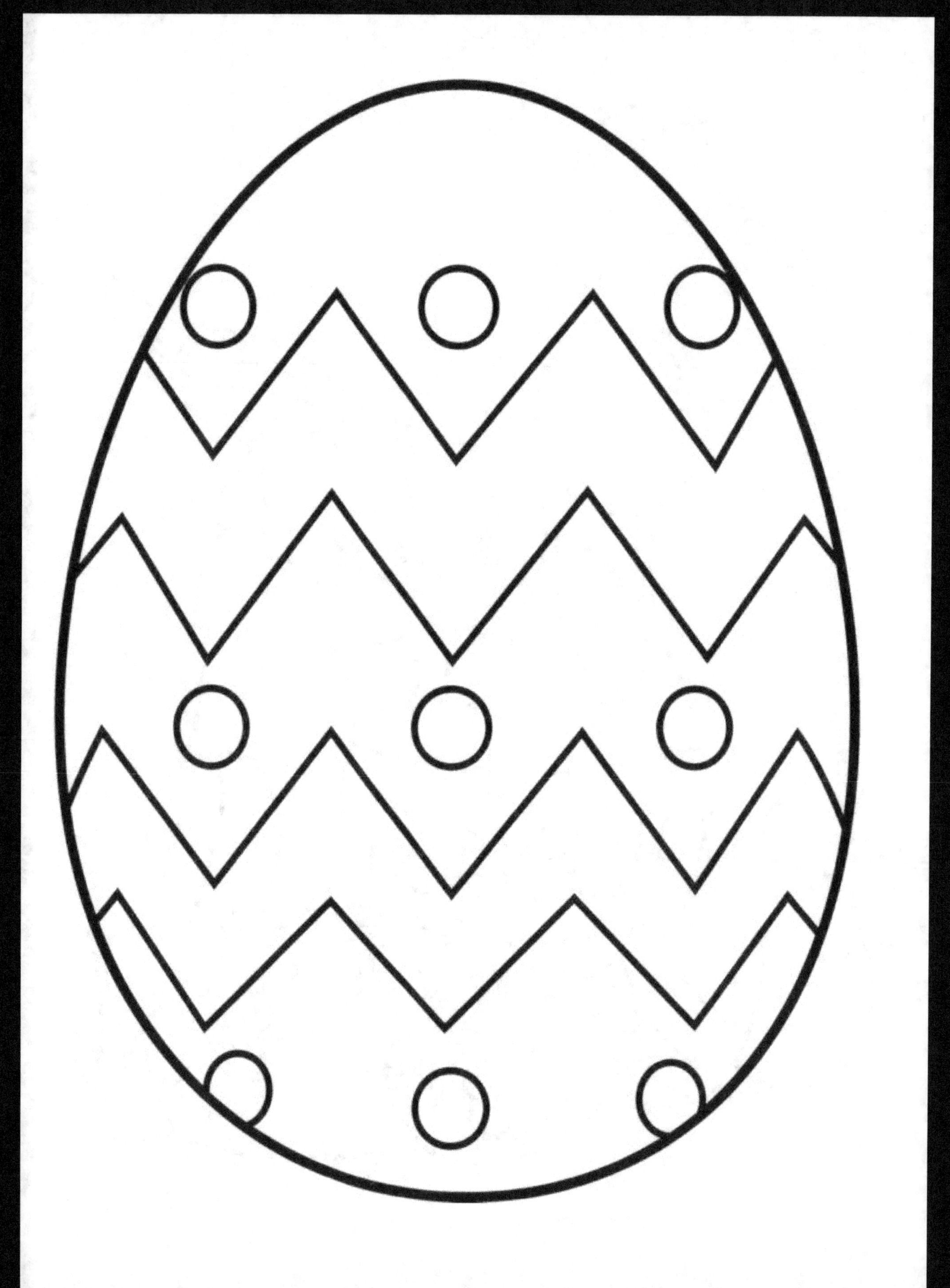

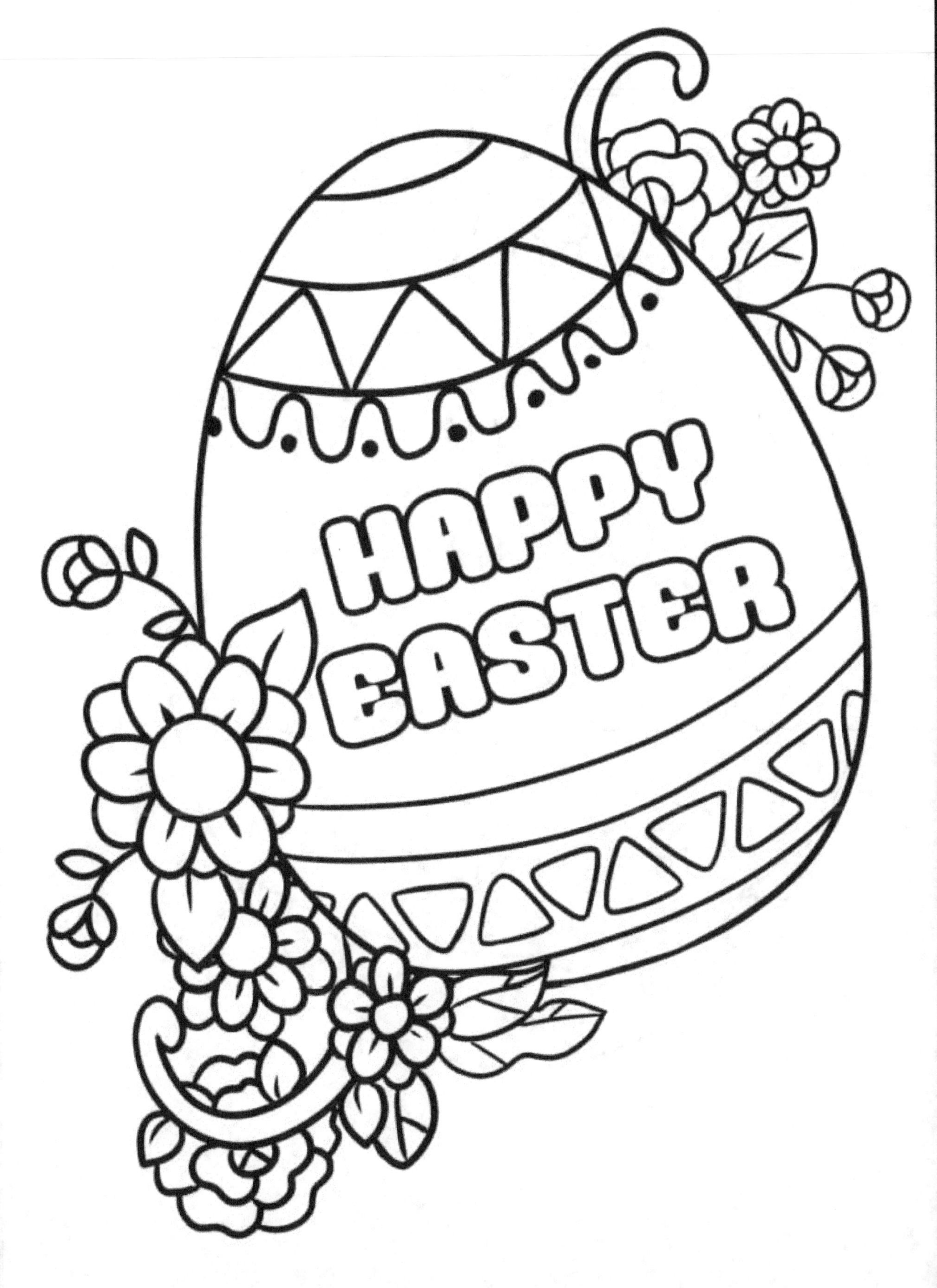

HAPPY
EASTER

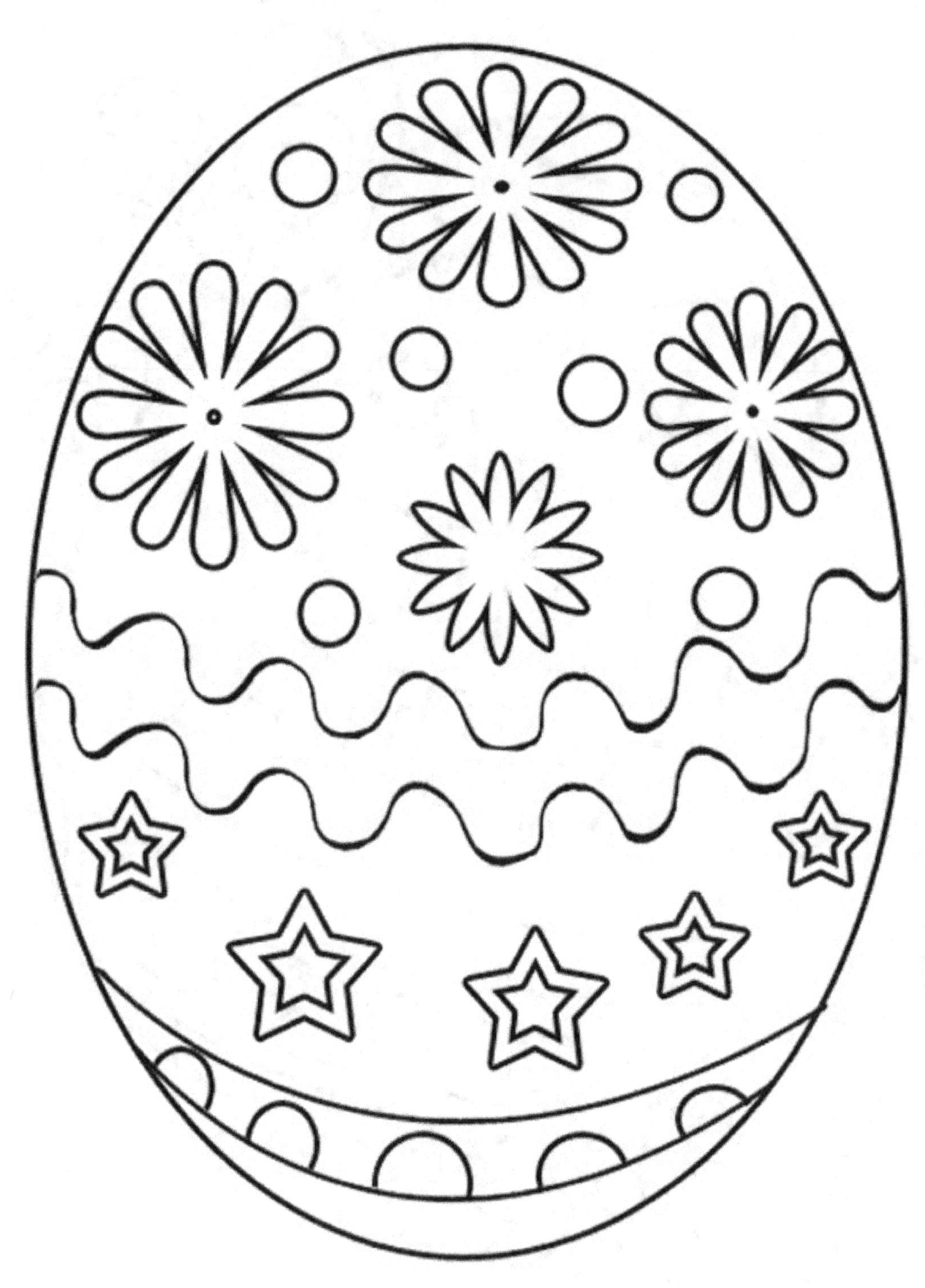

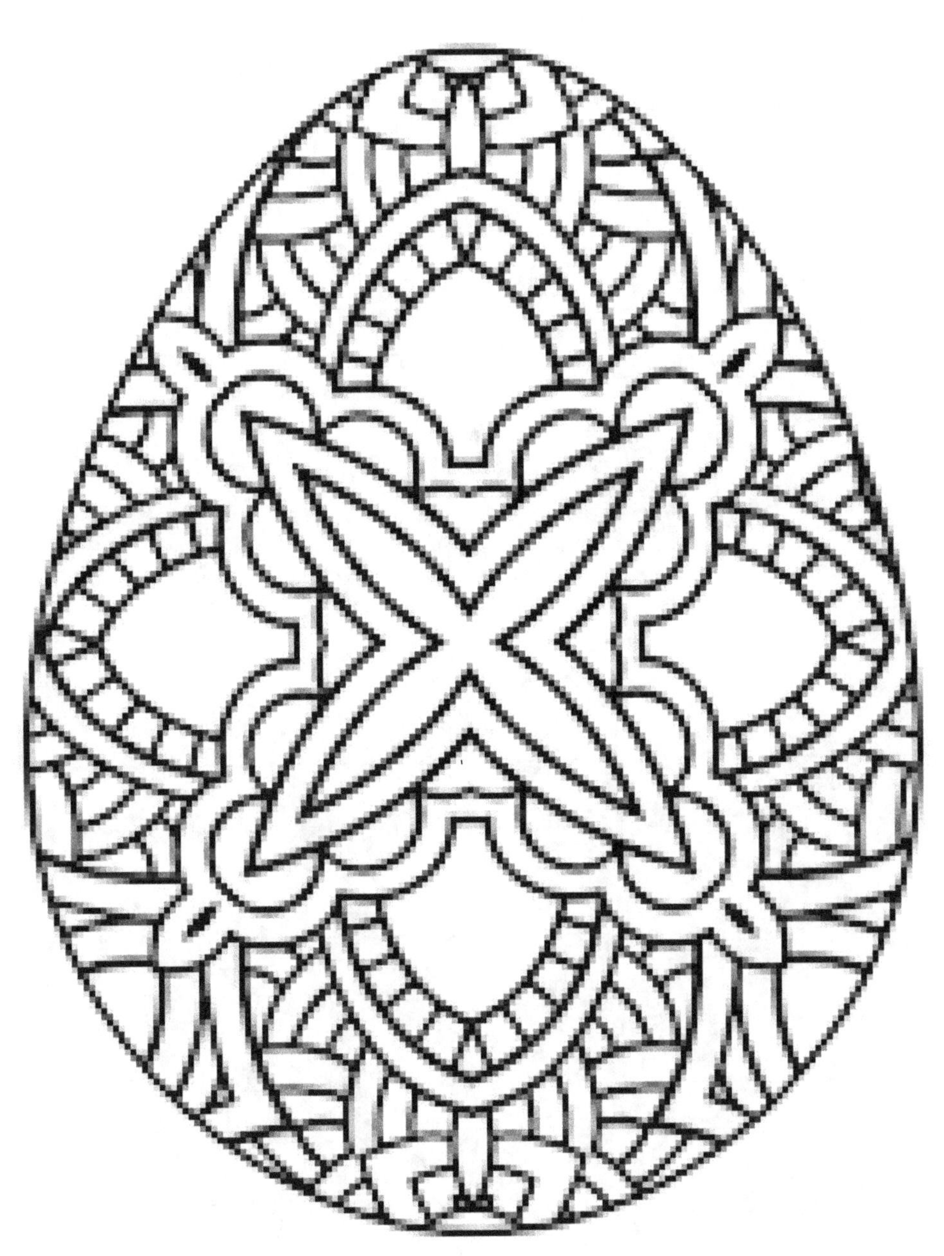

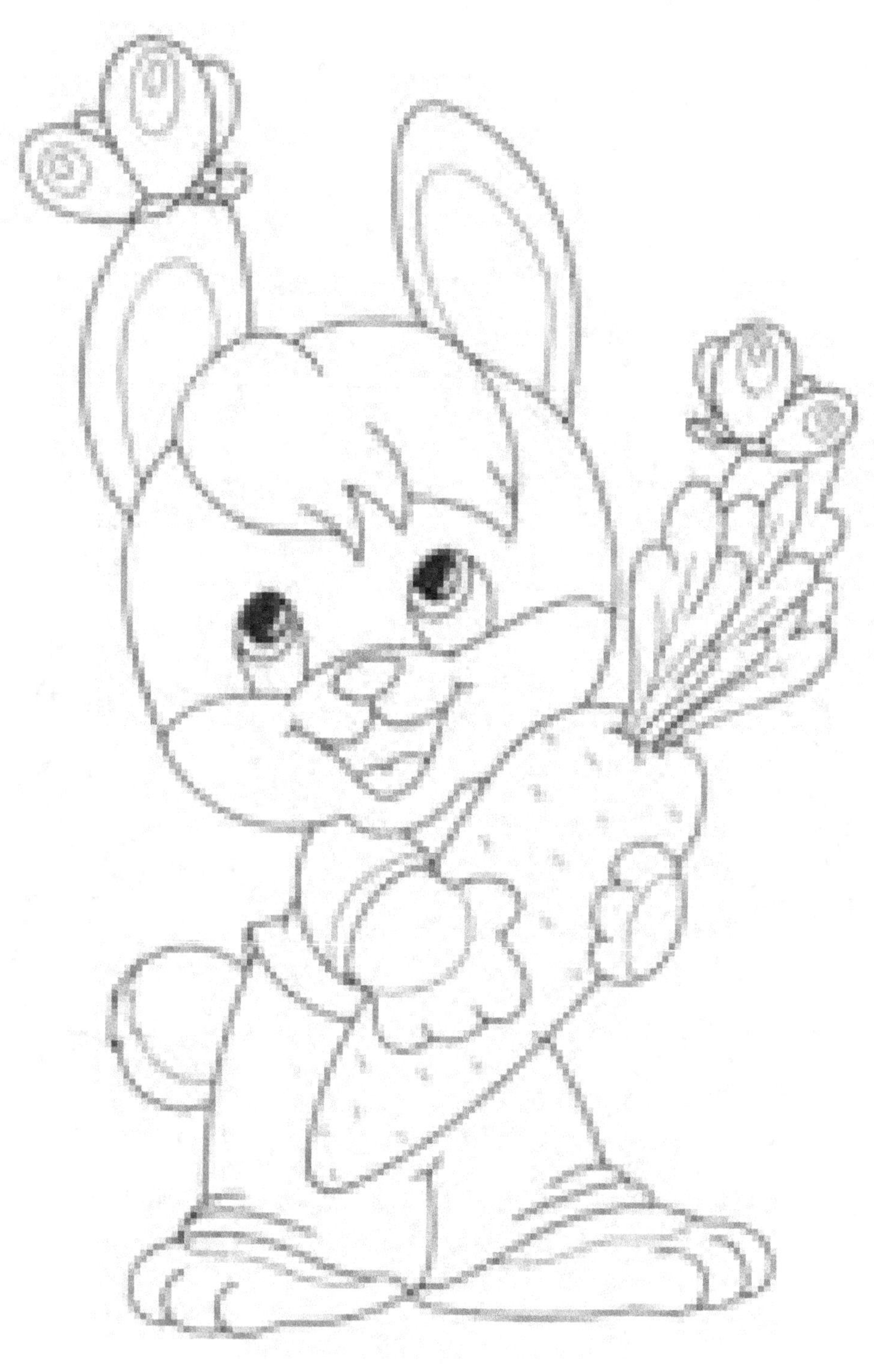

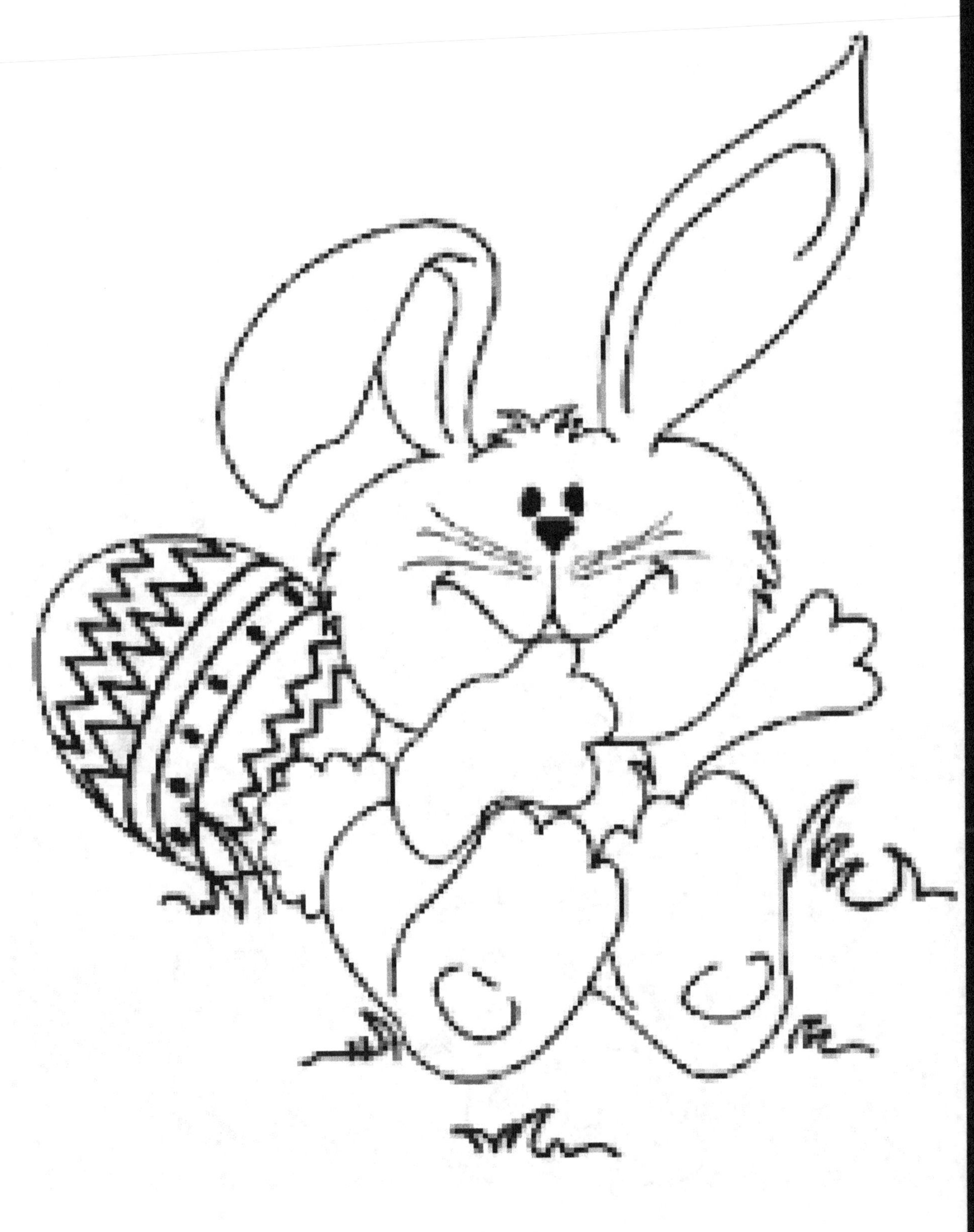

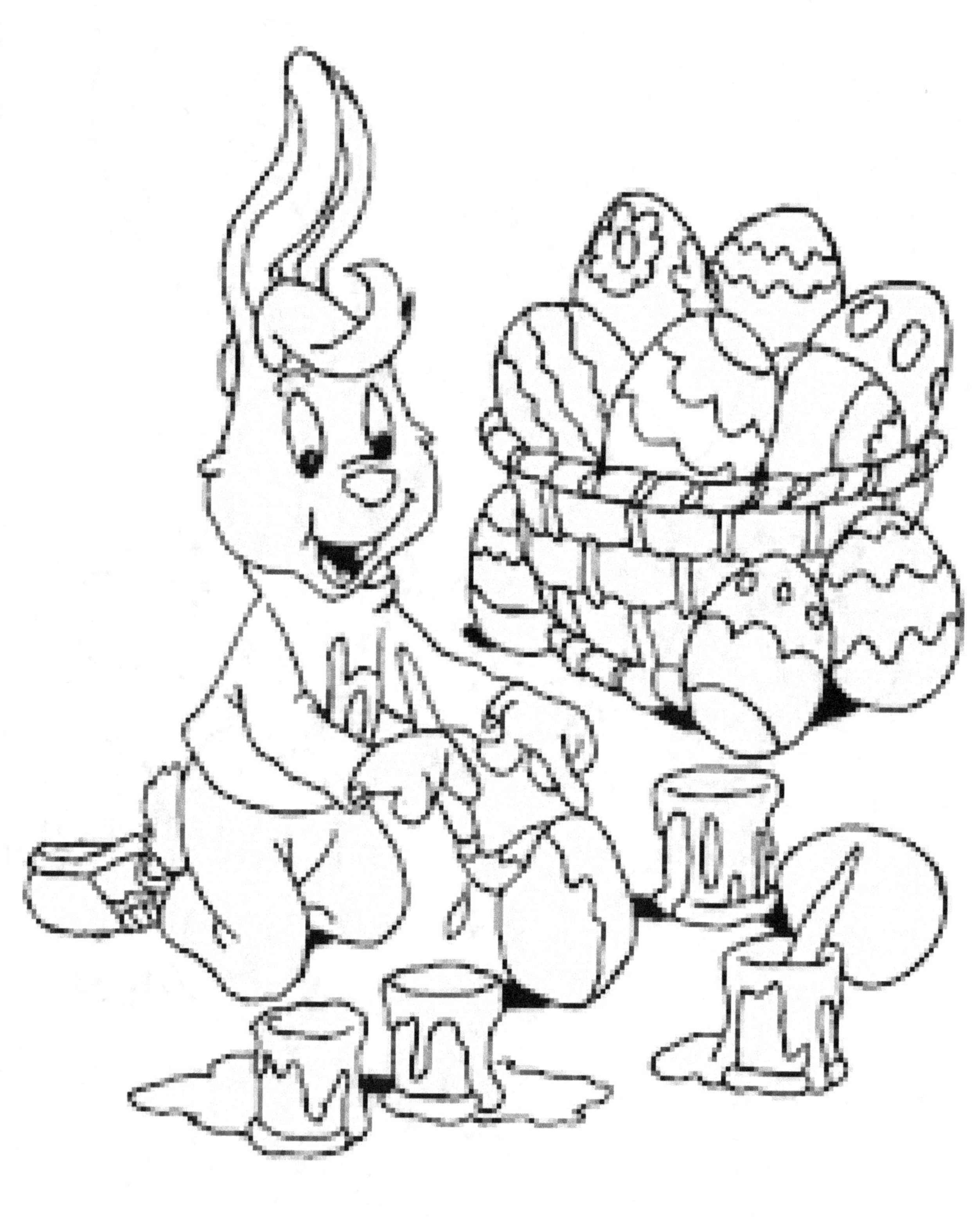

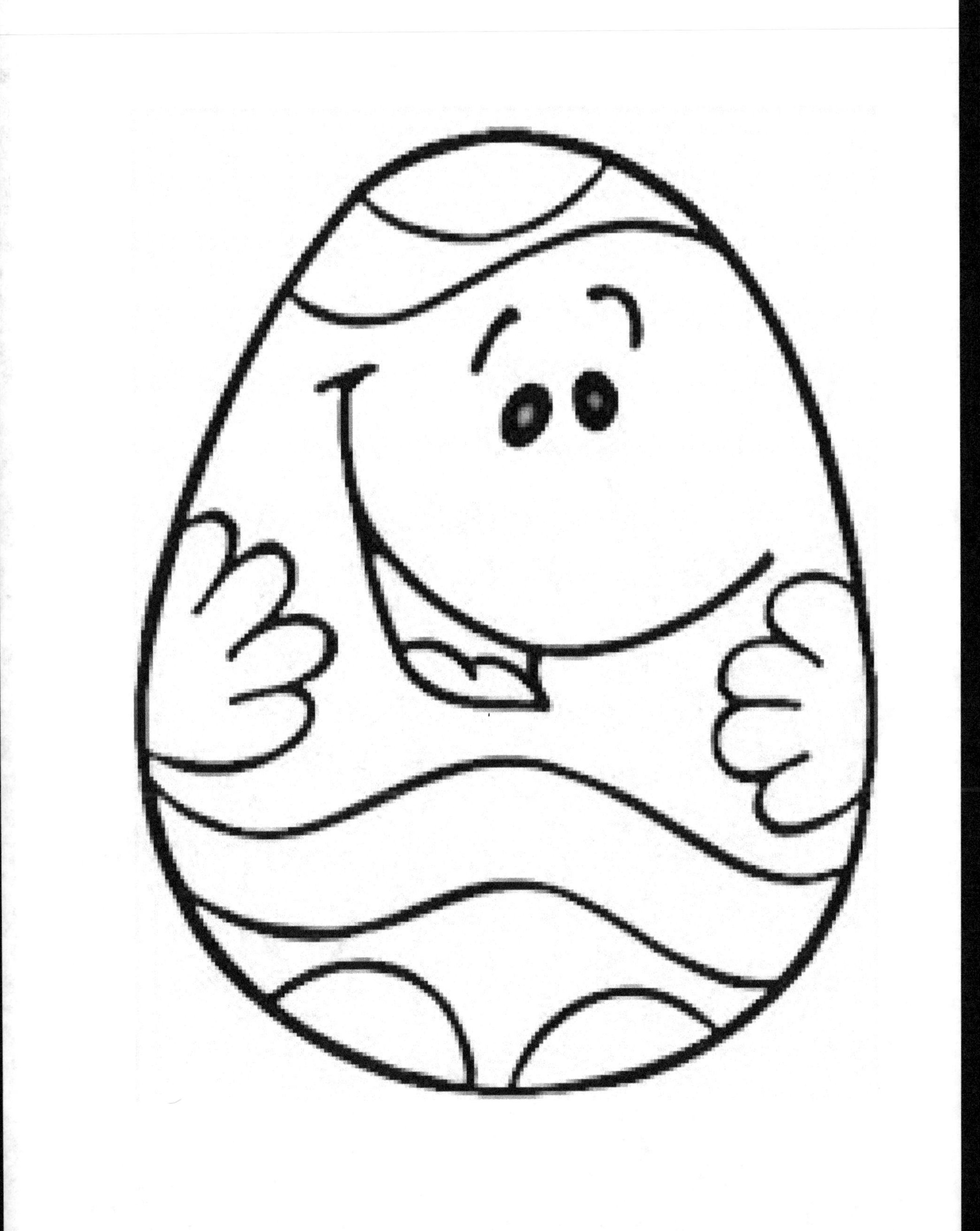

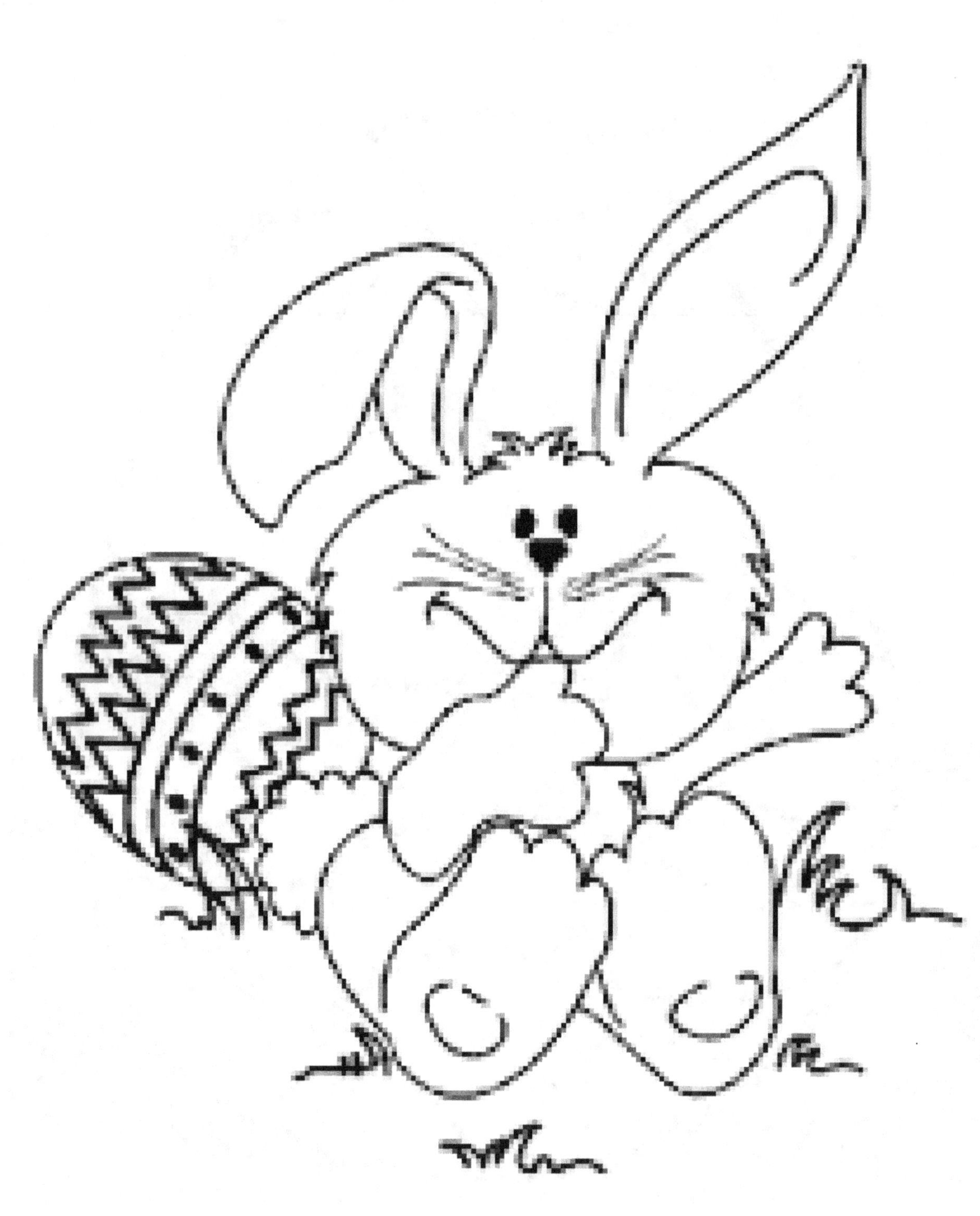

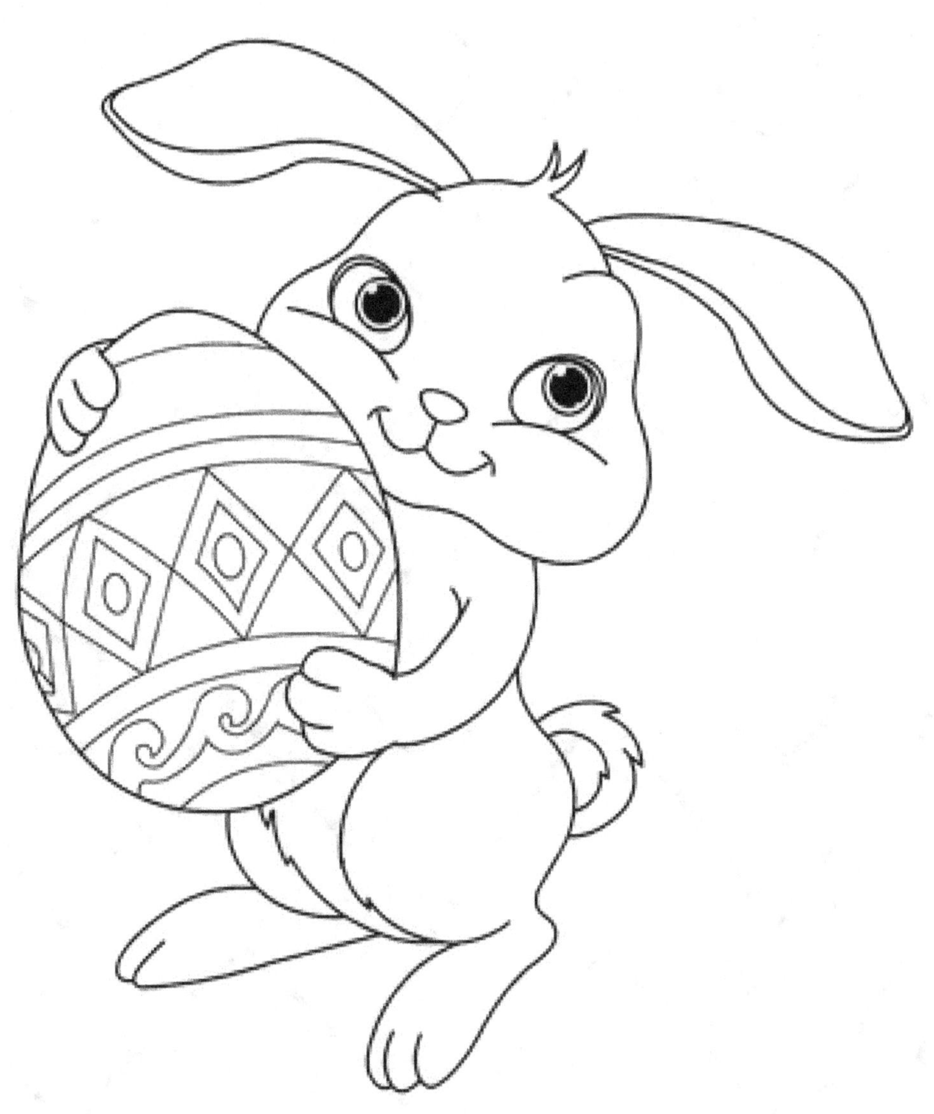

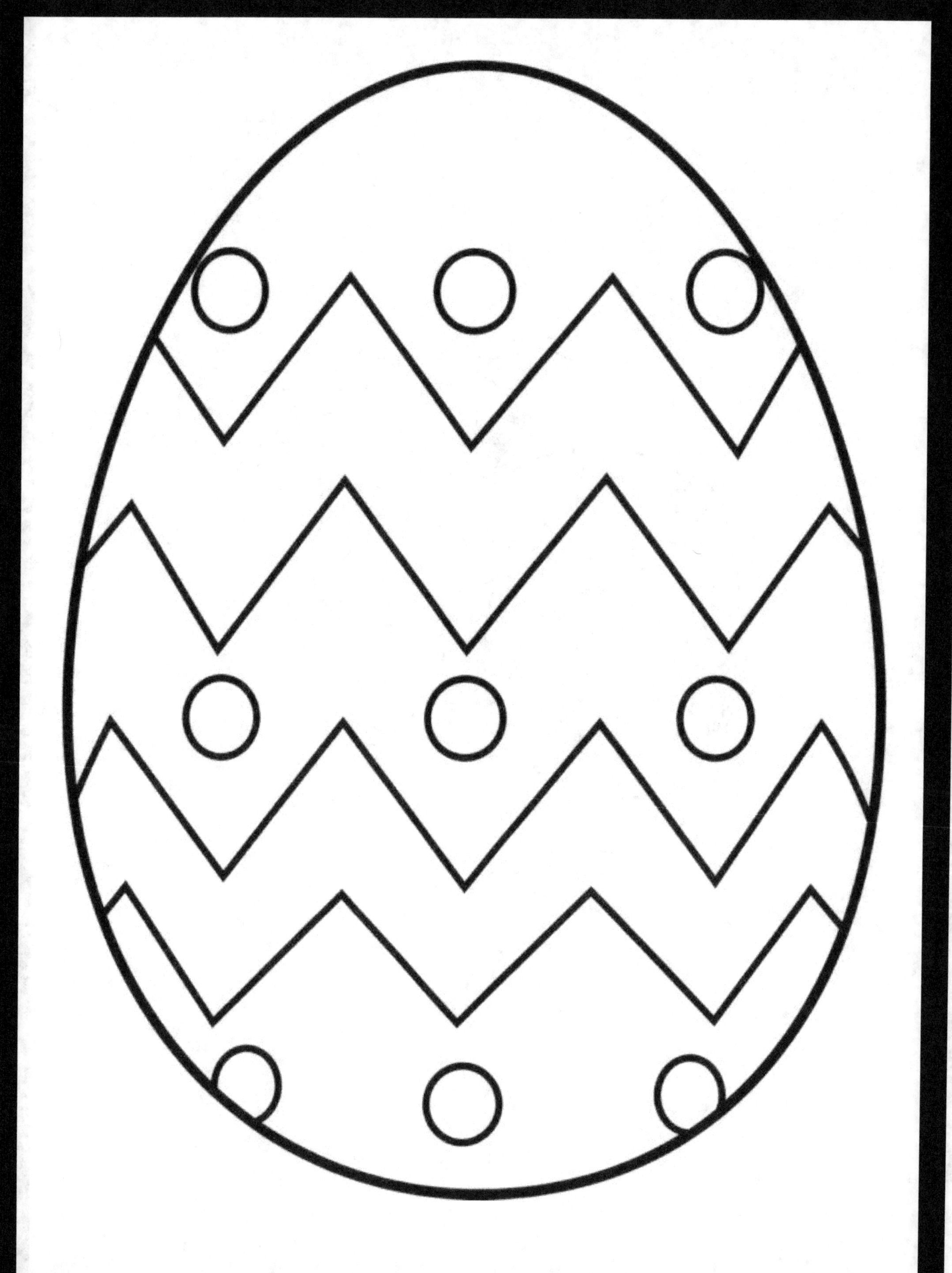

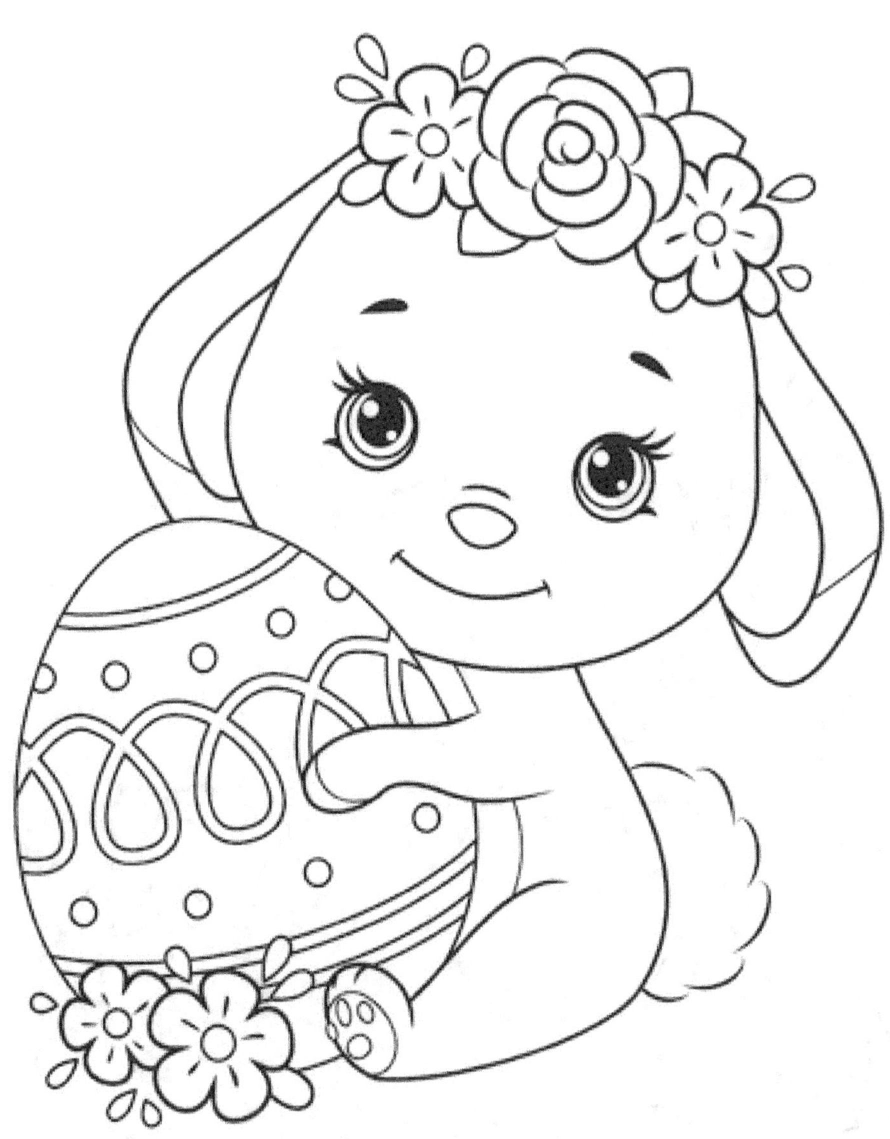

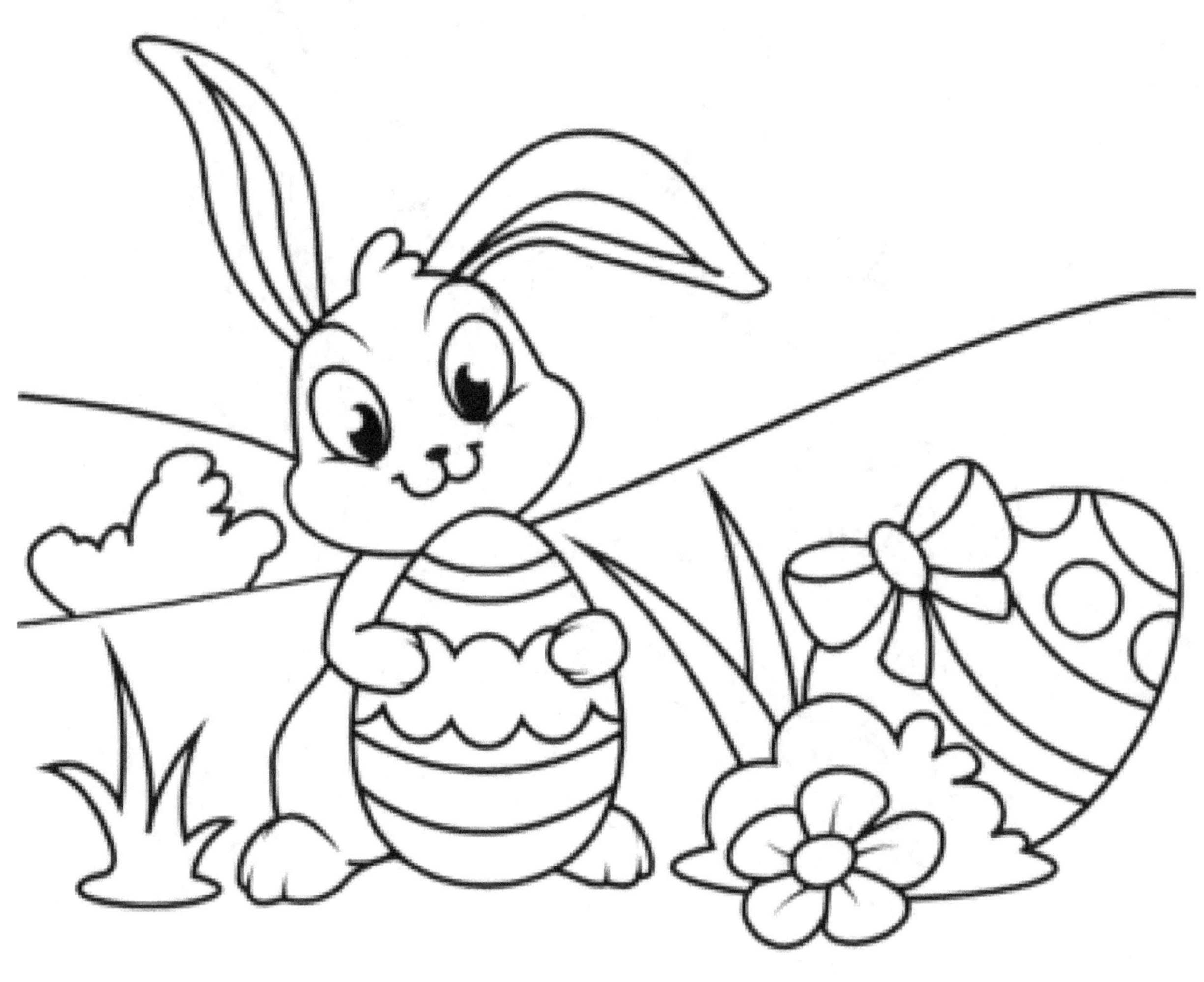

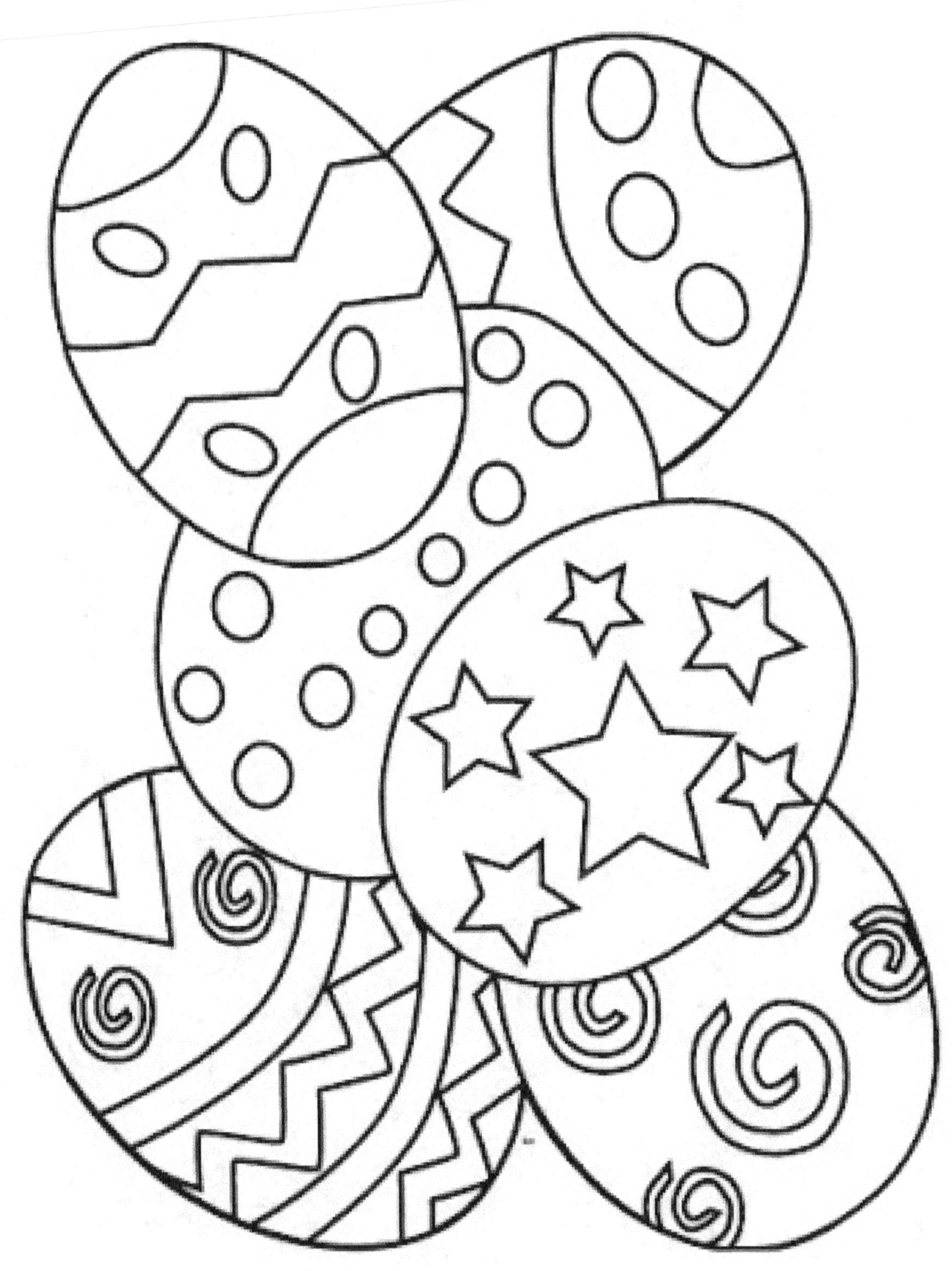

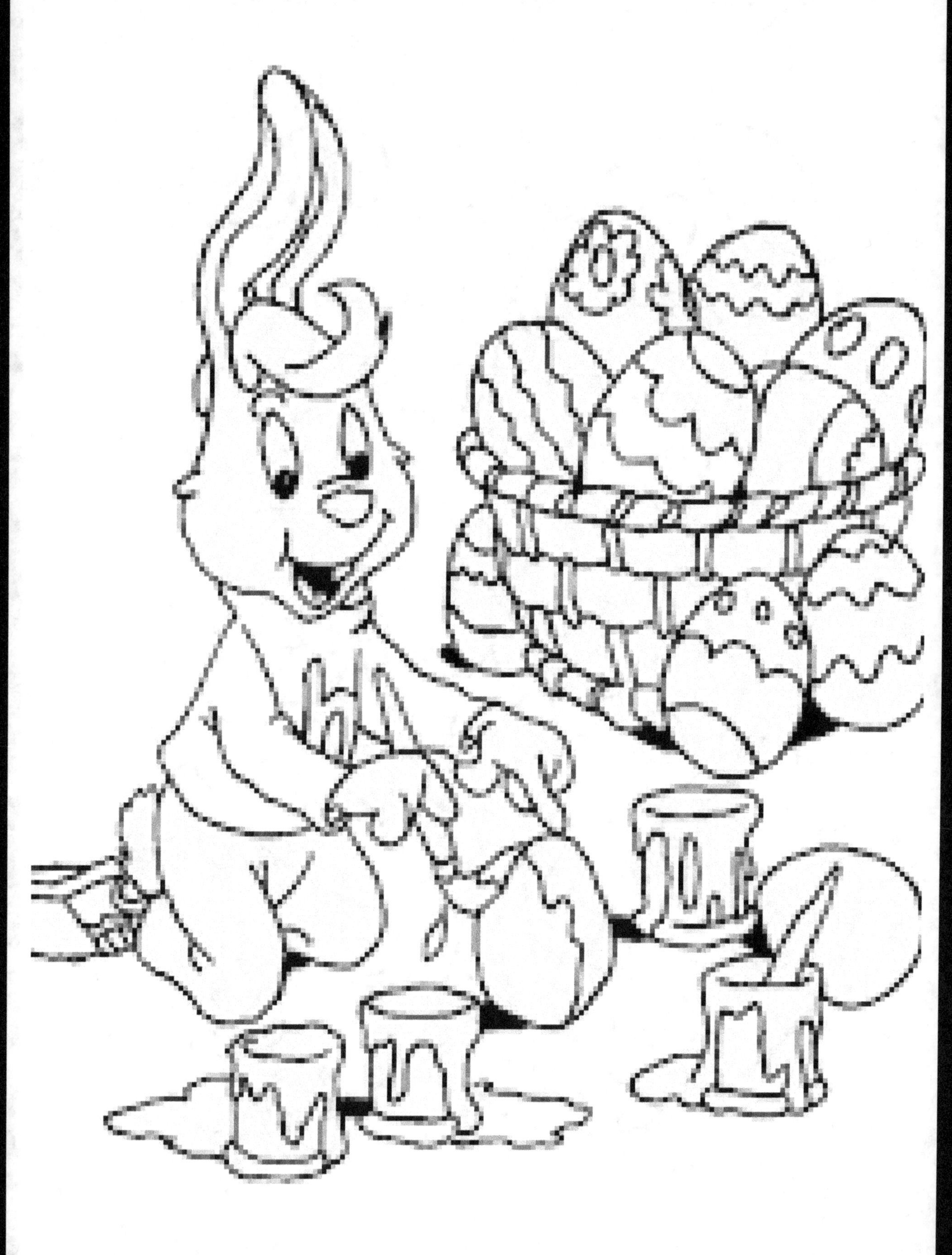

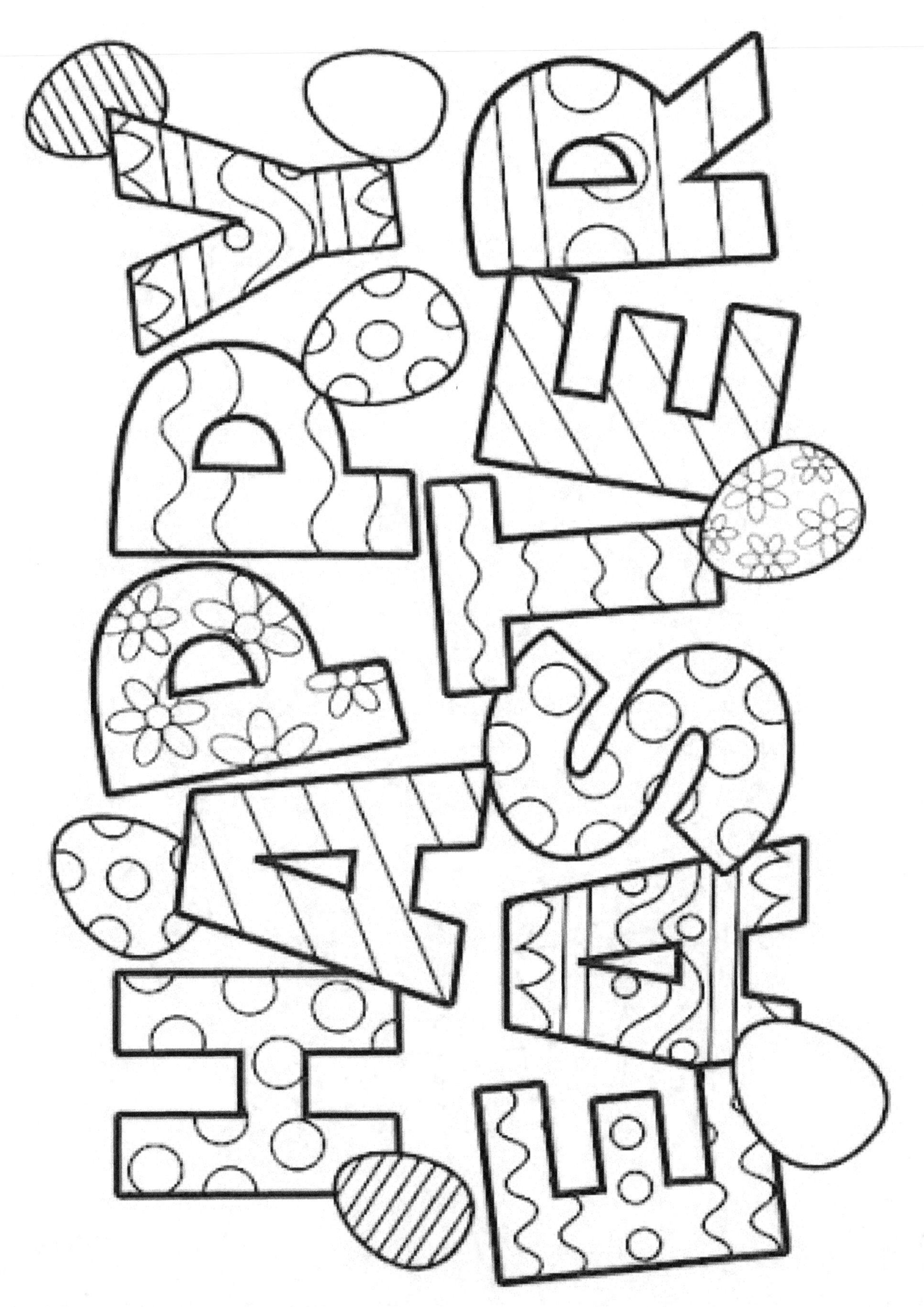

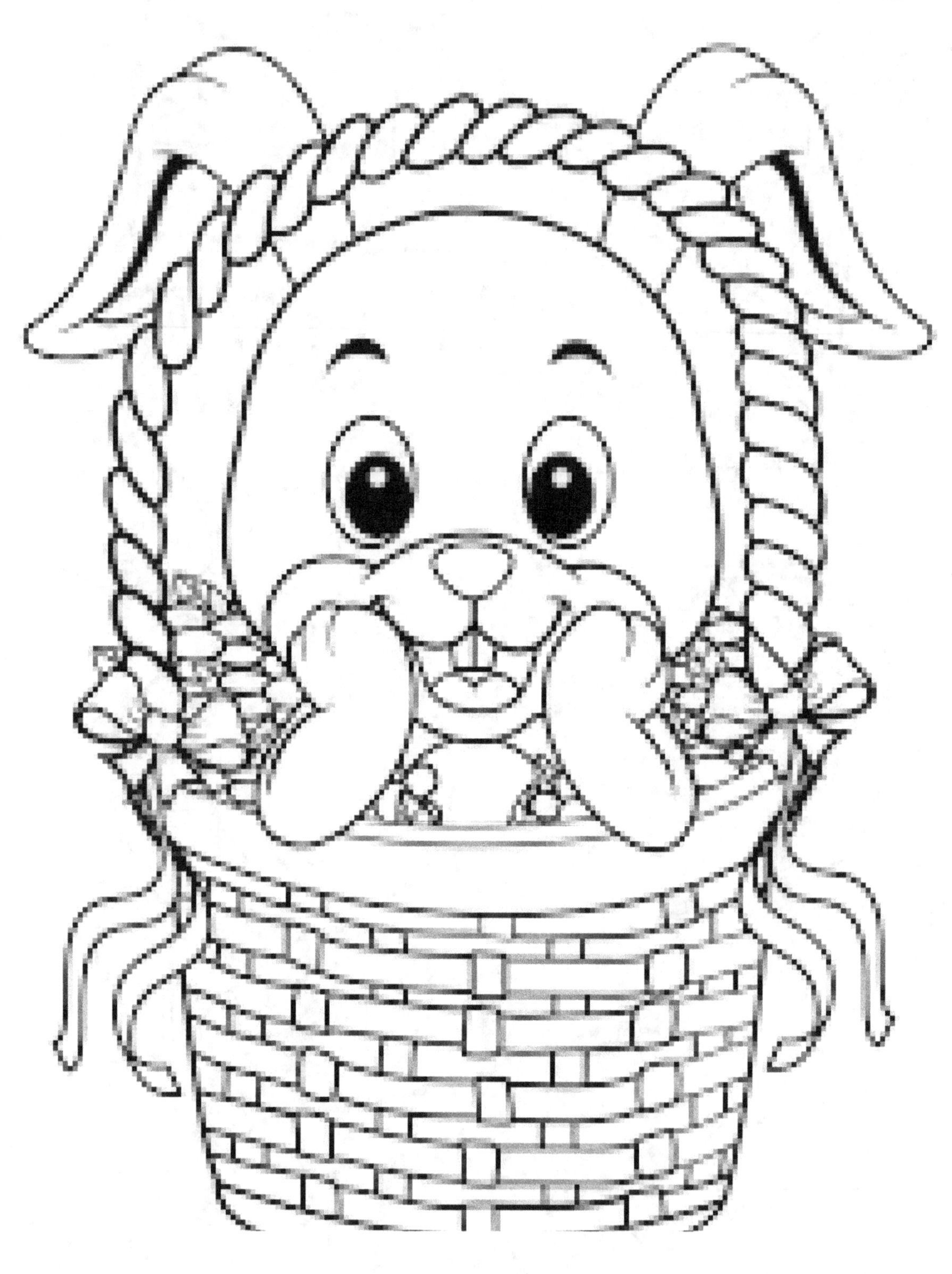

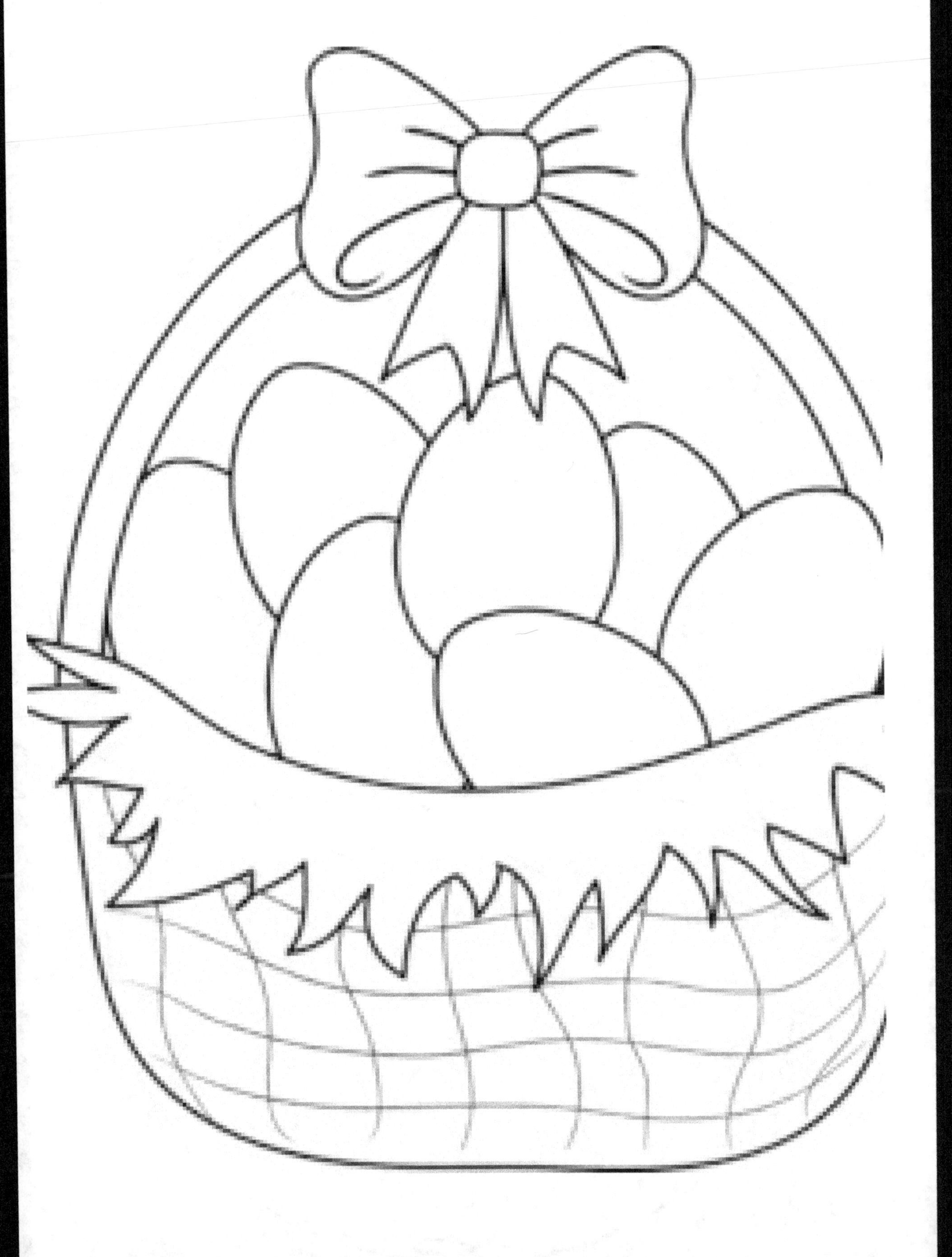

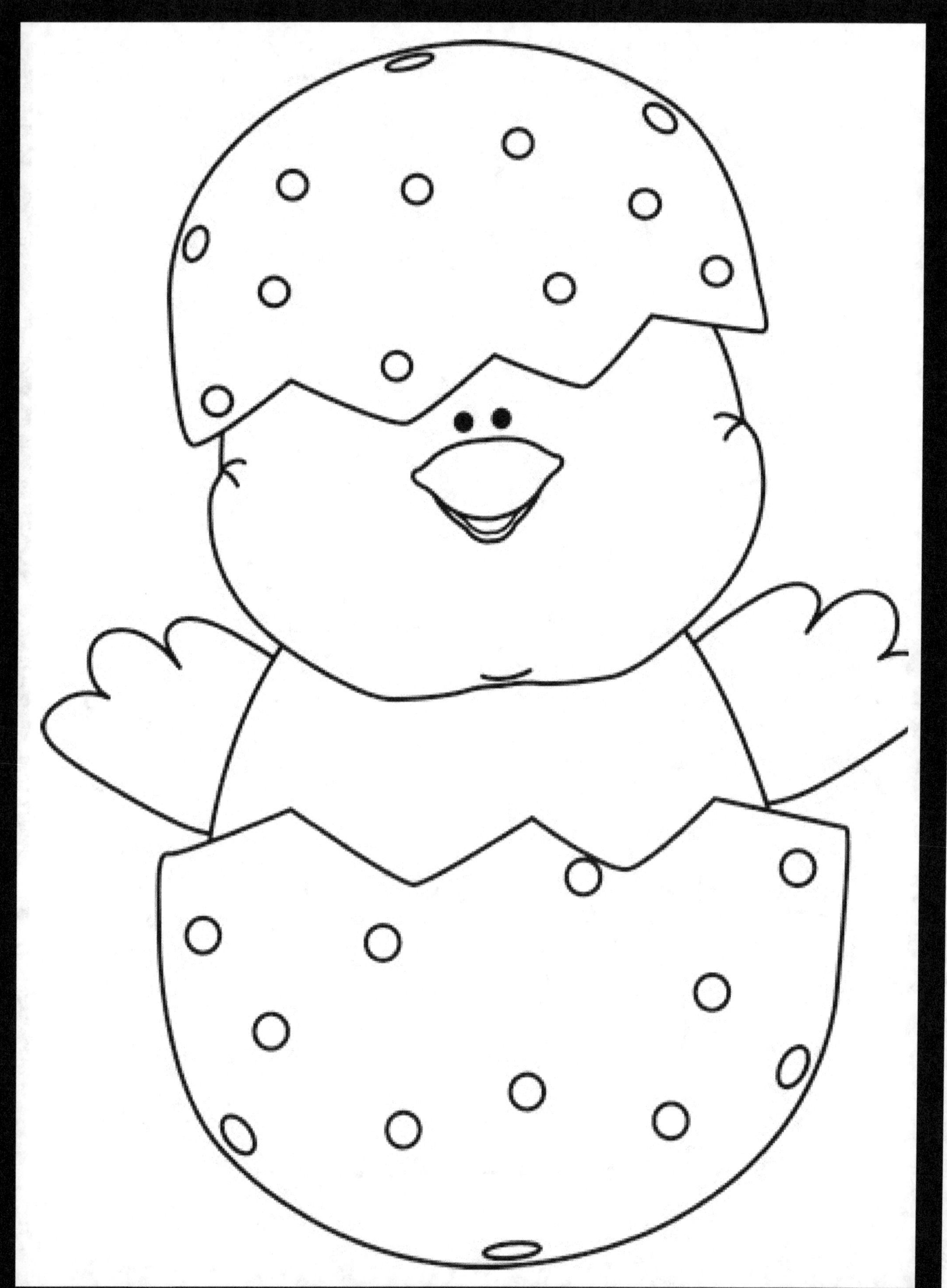

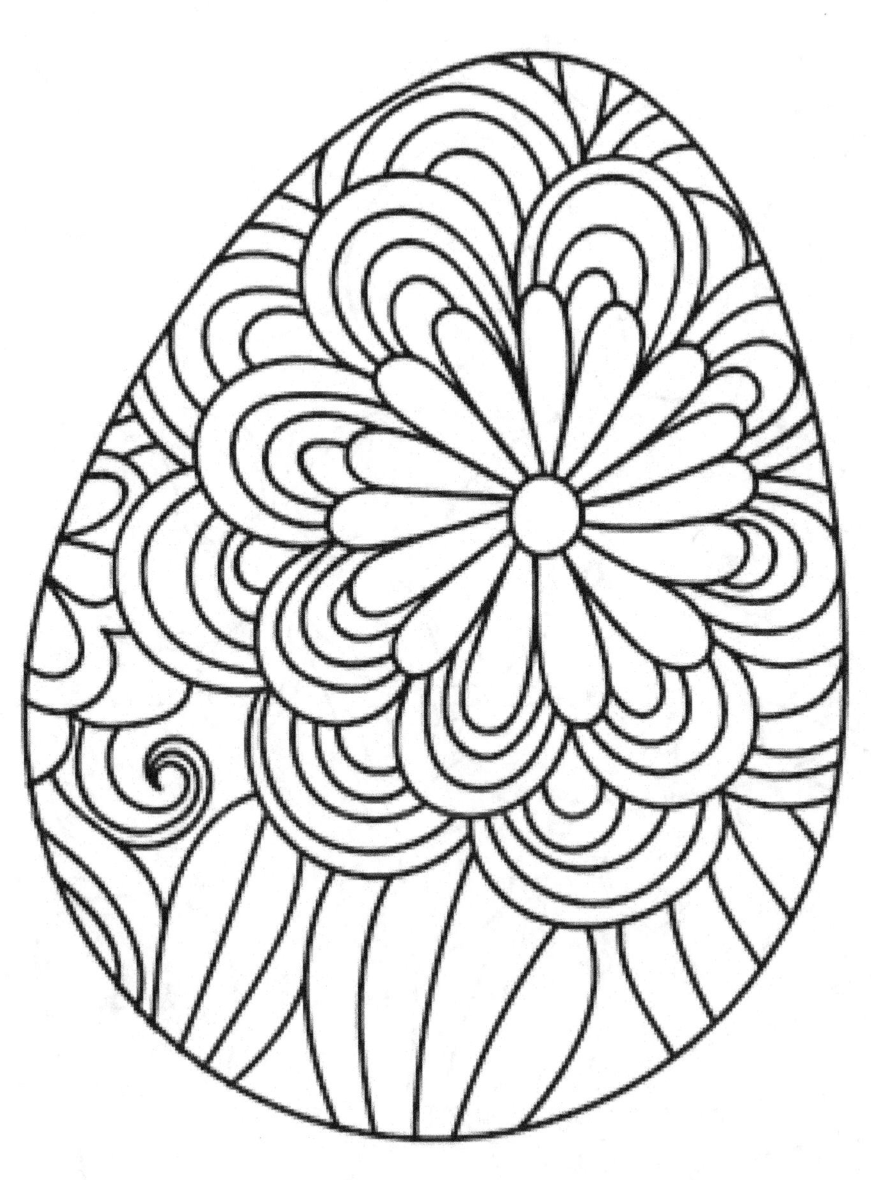

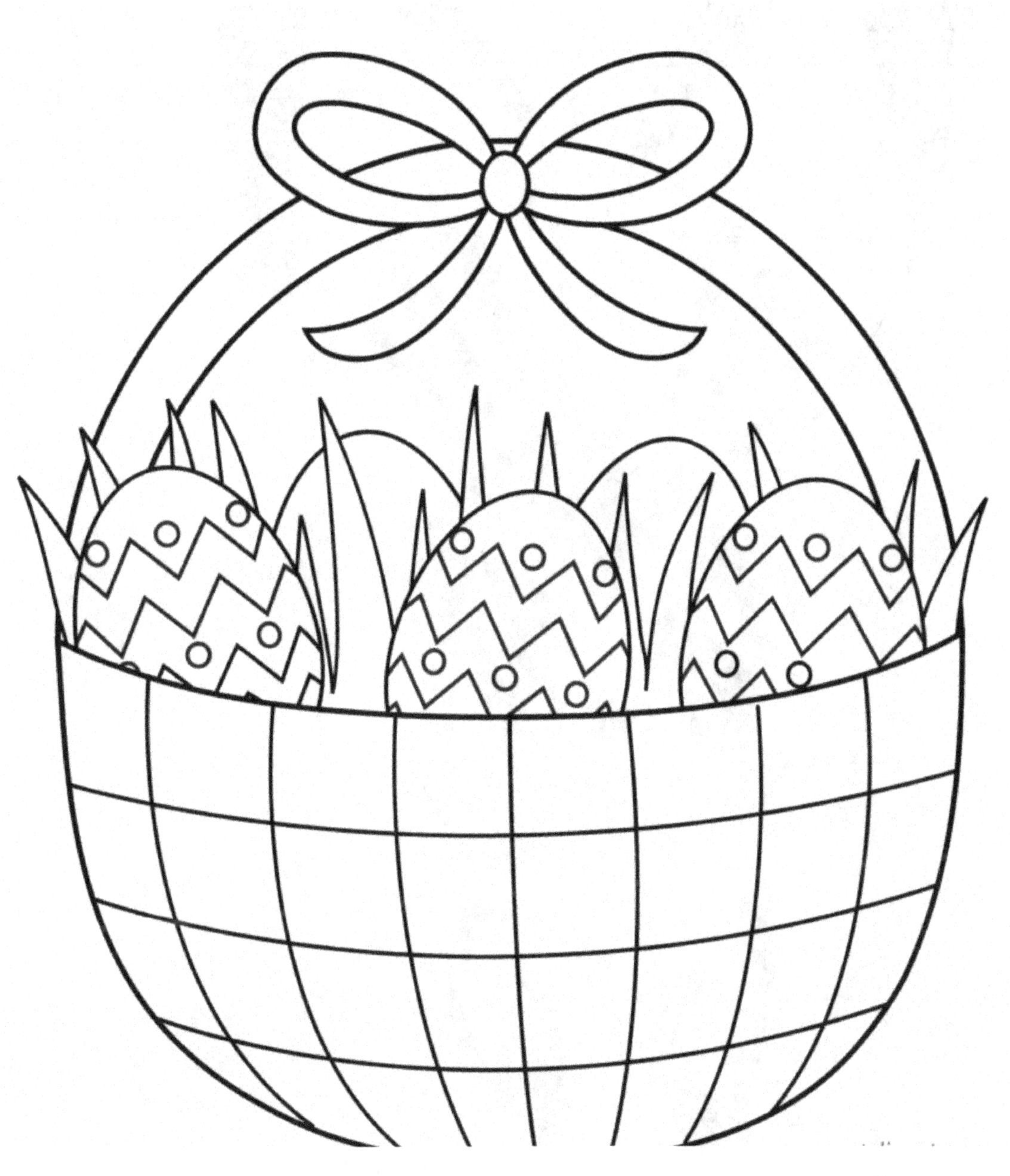

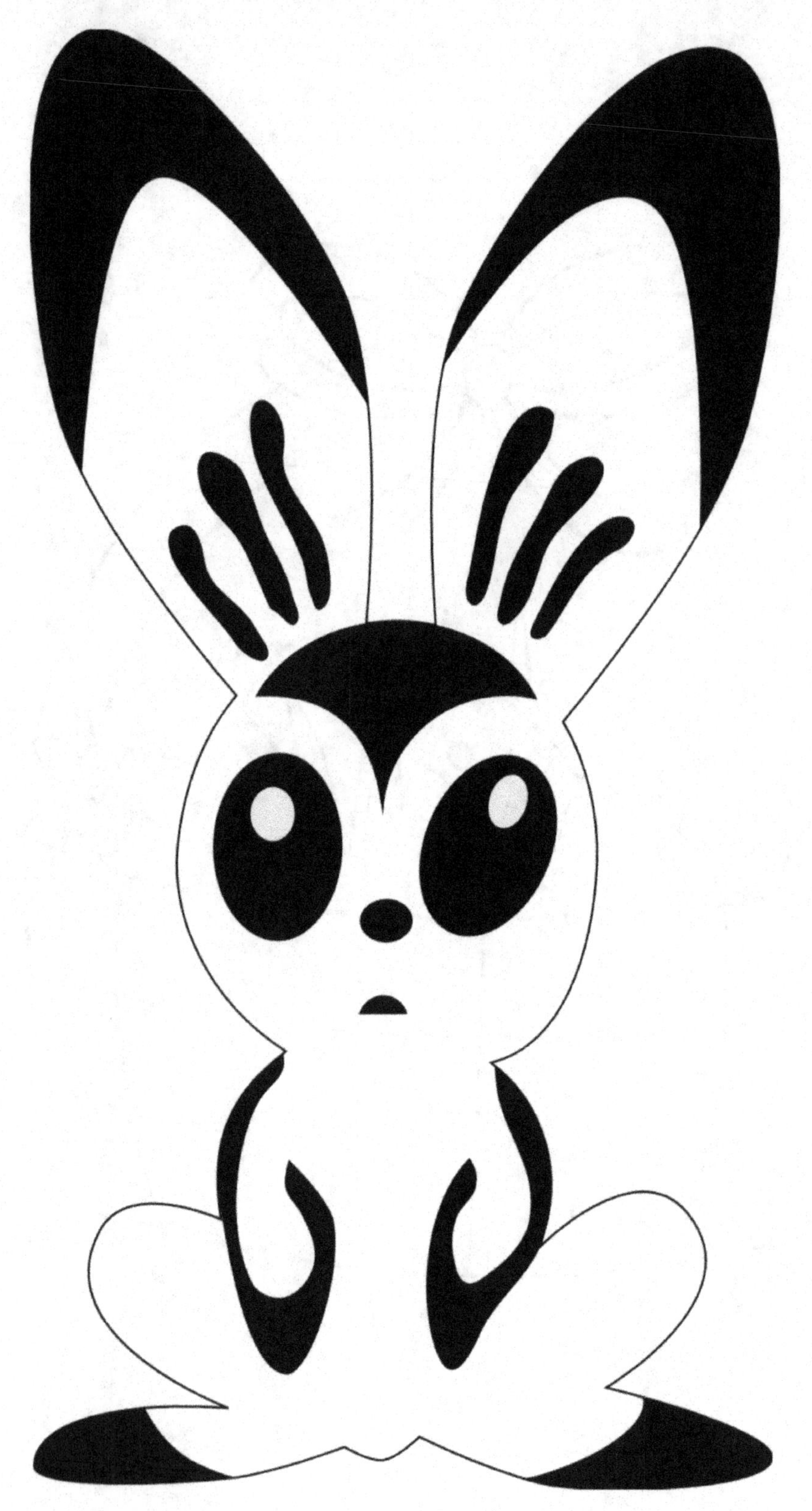

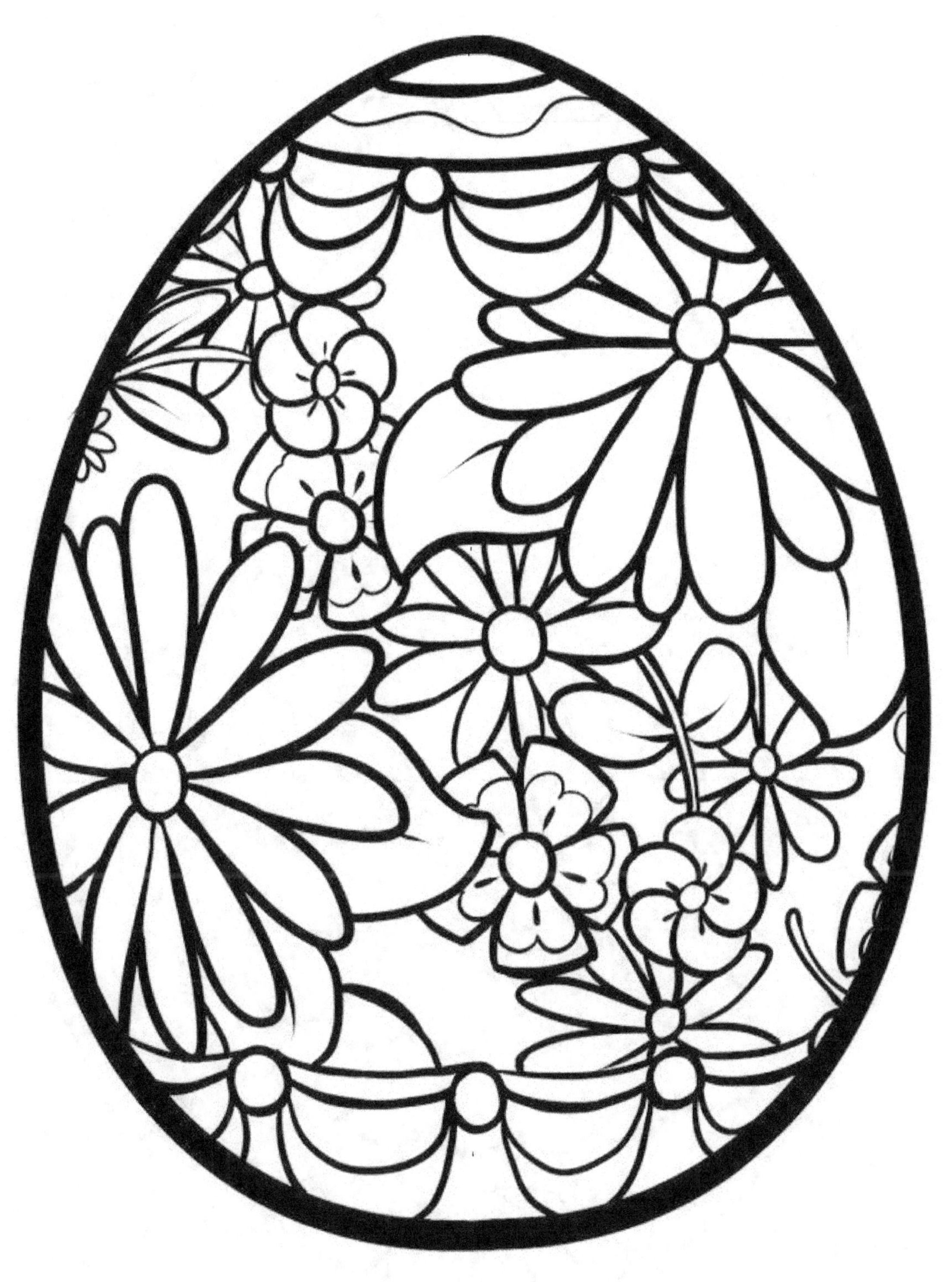

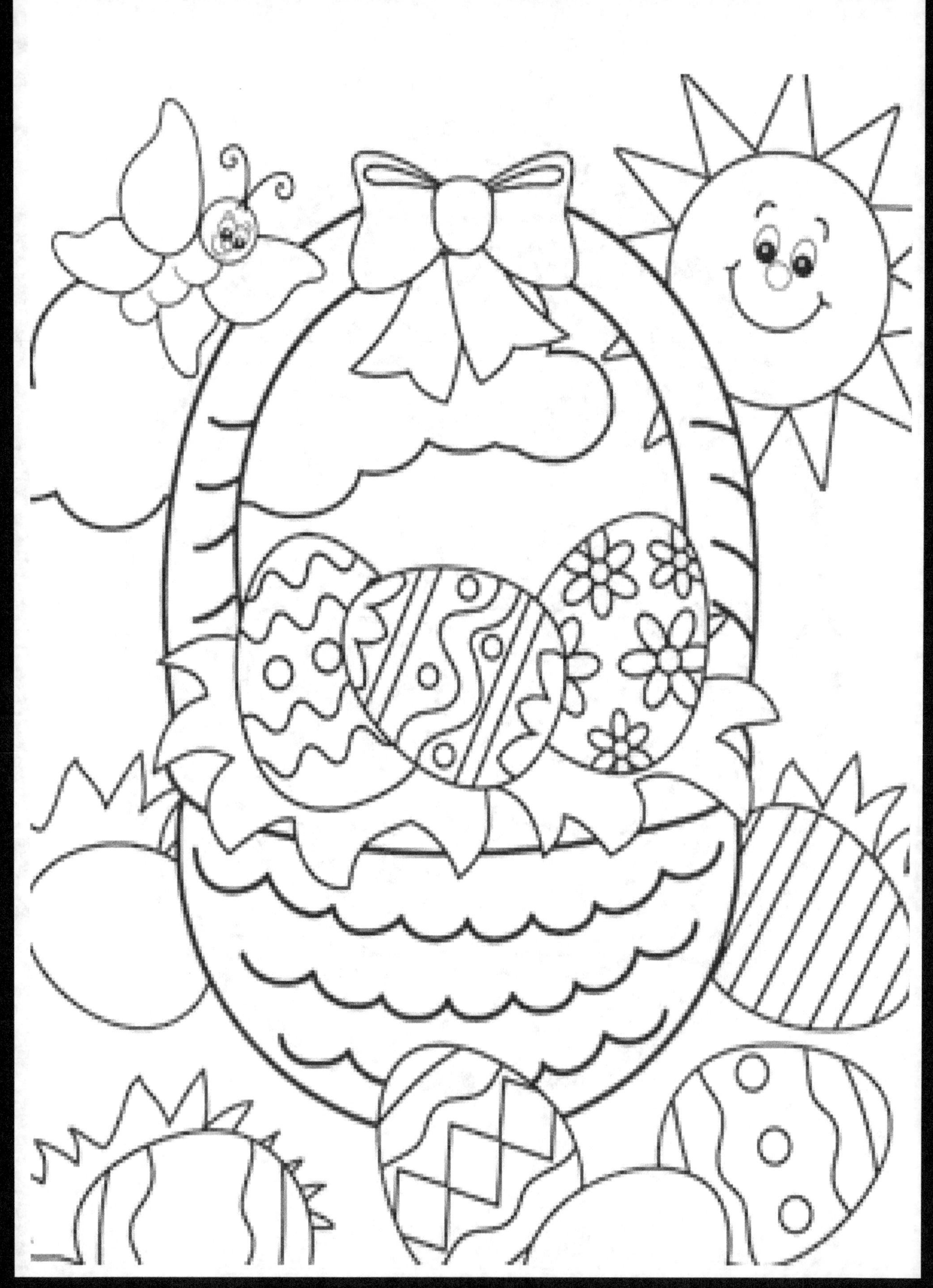

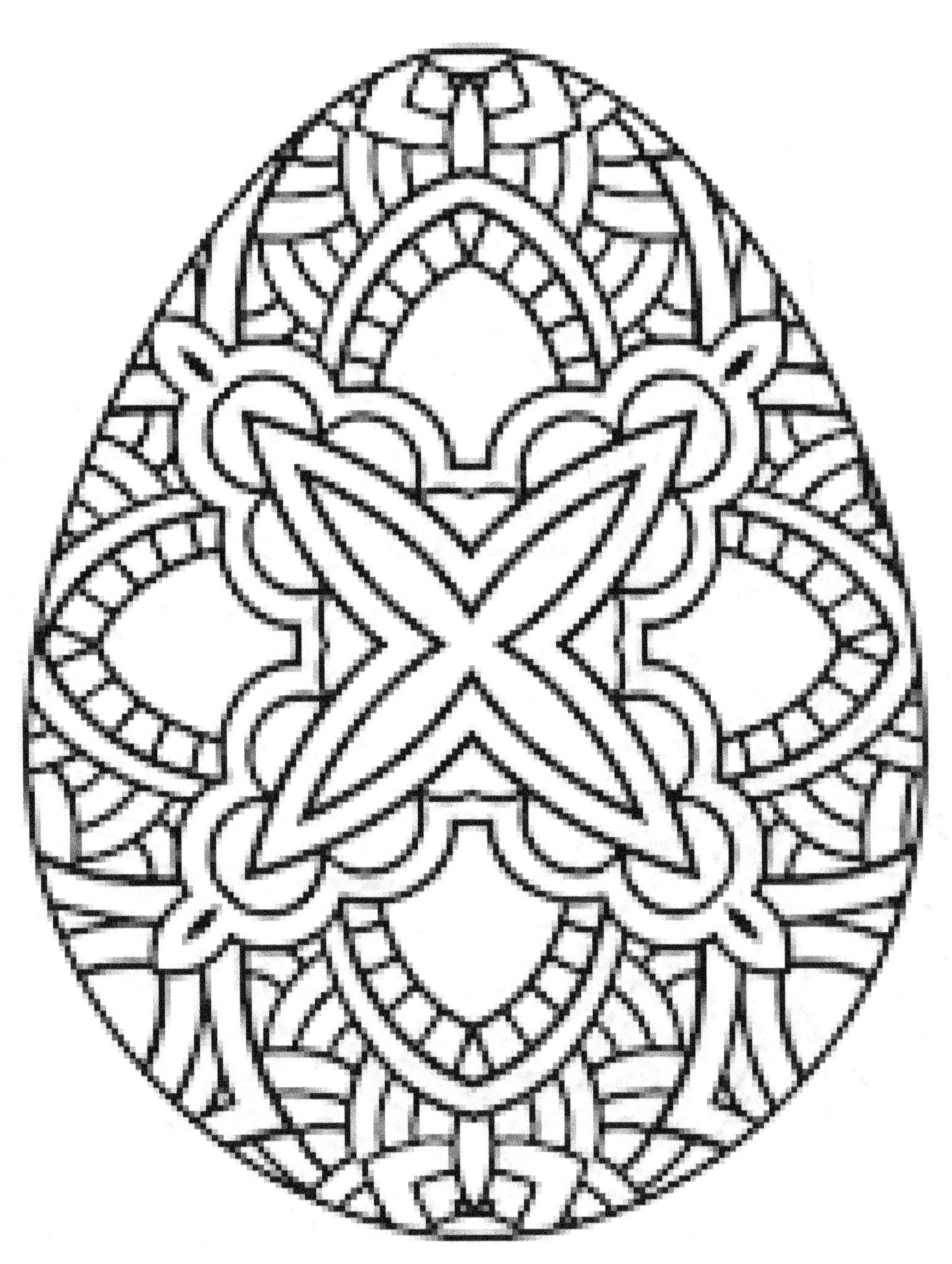

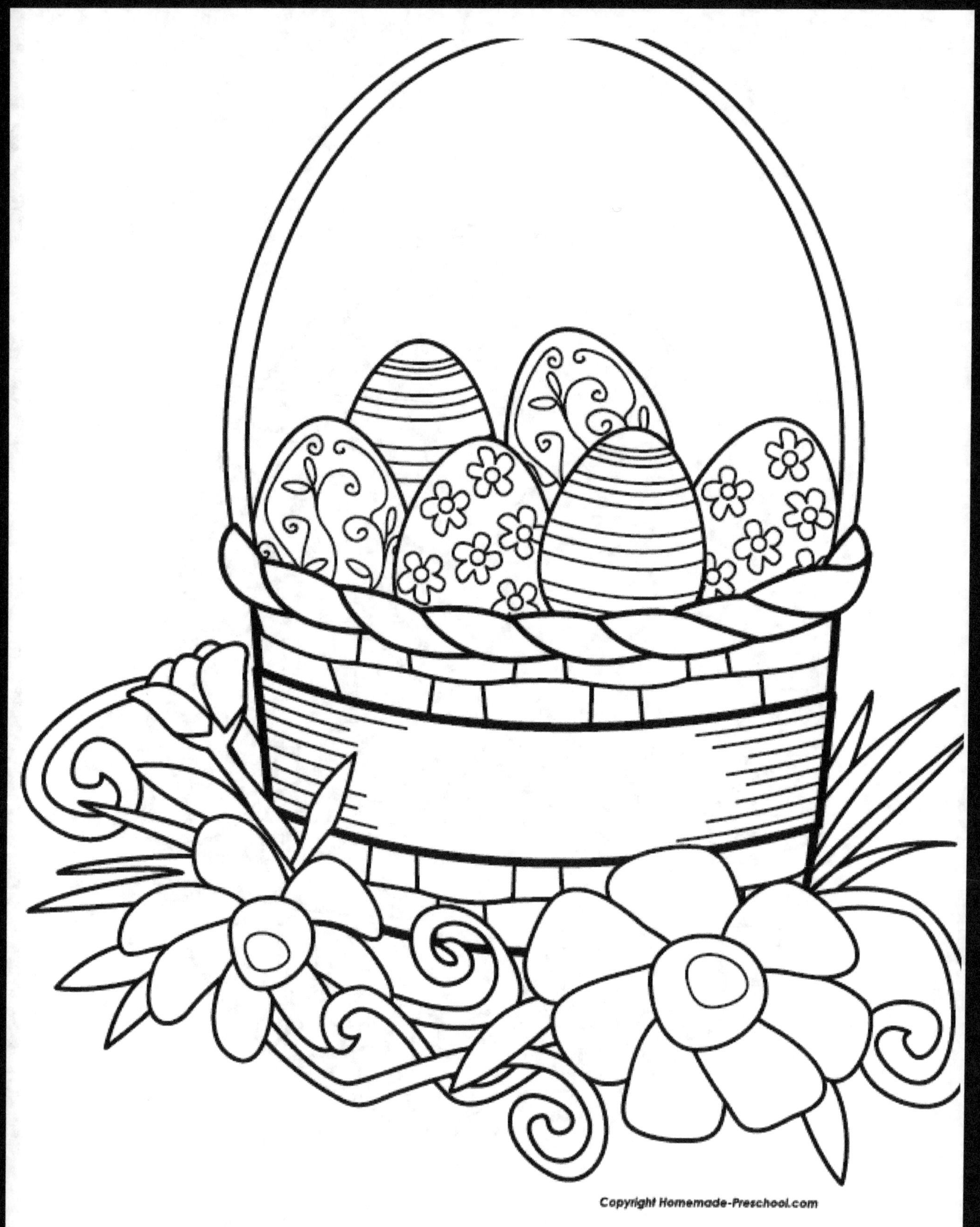

Copyright Homemade-Preschool.com

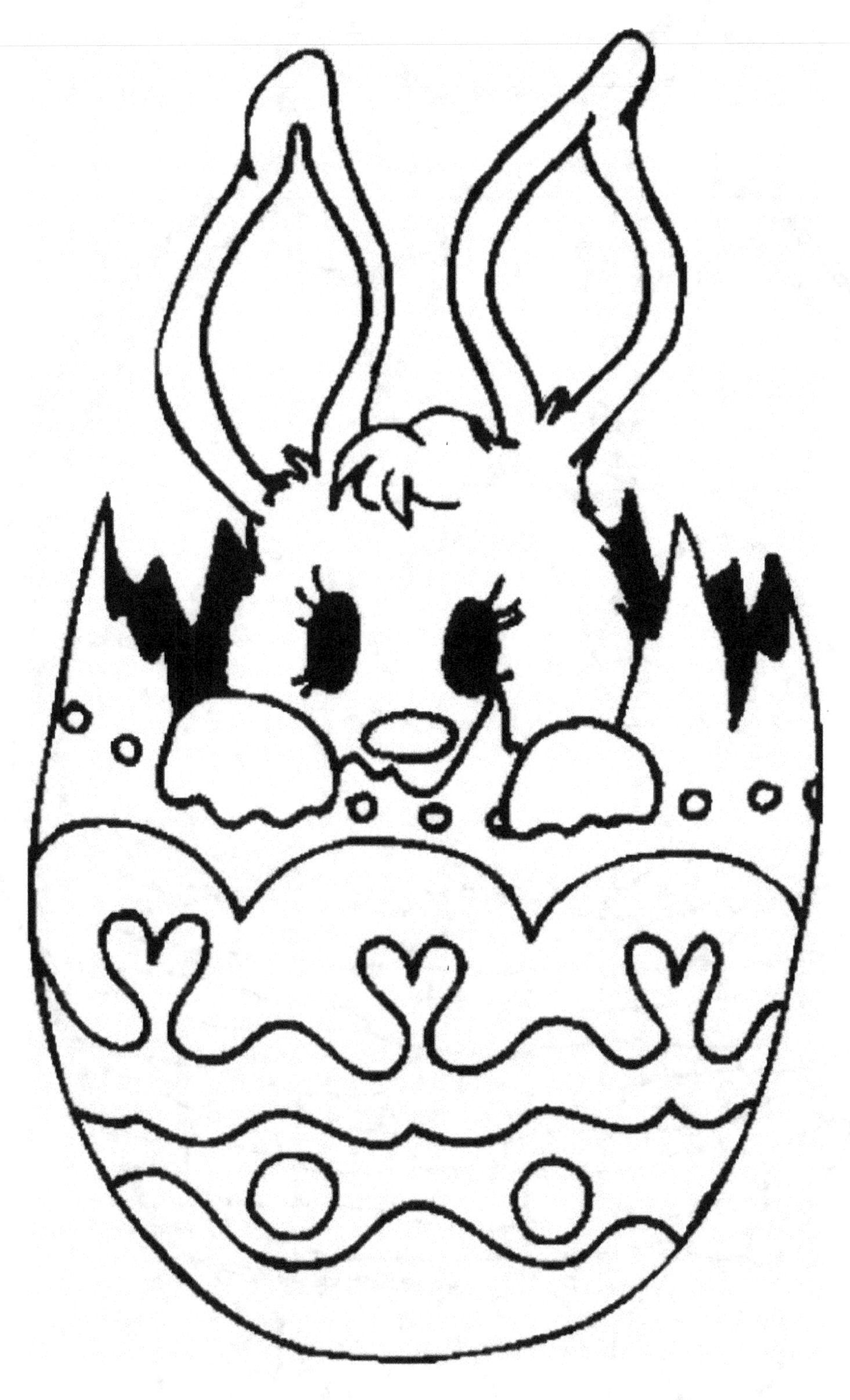

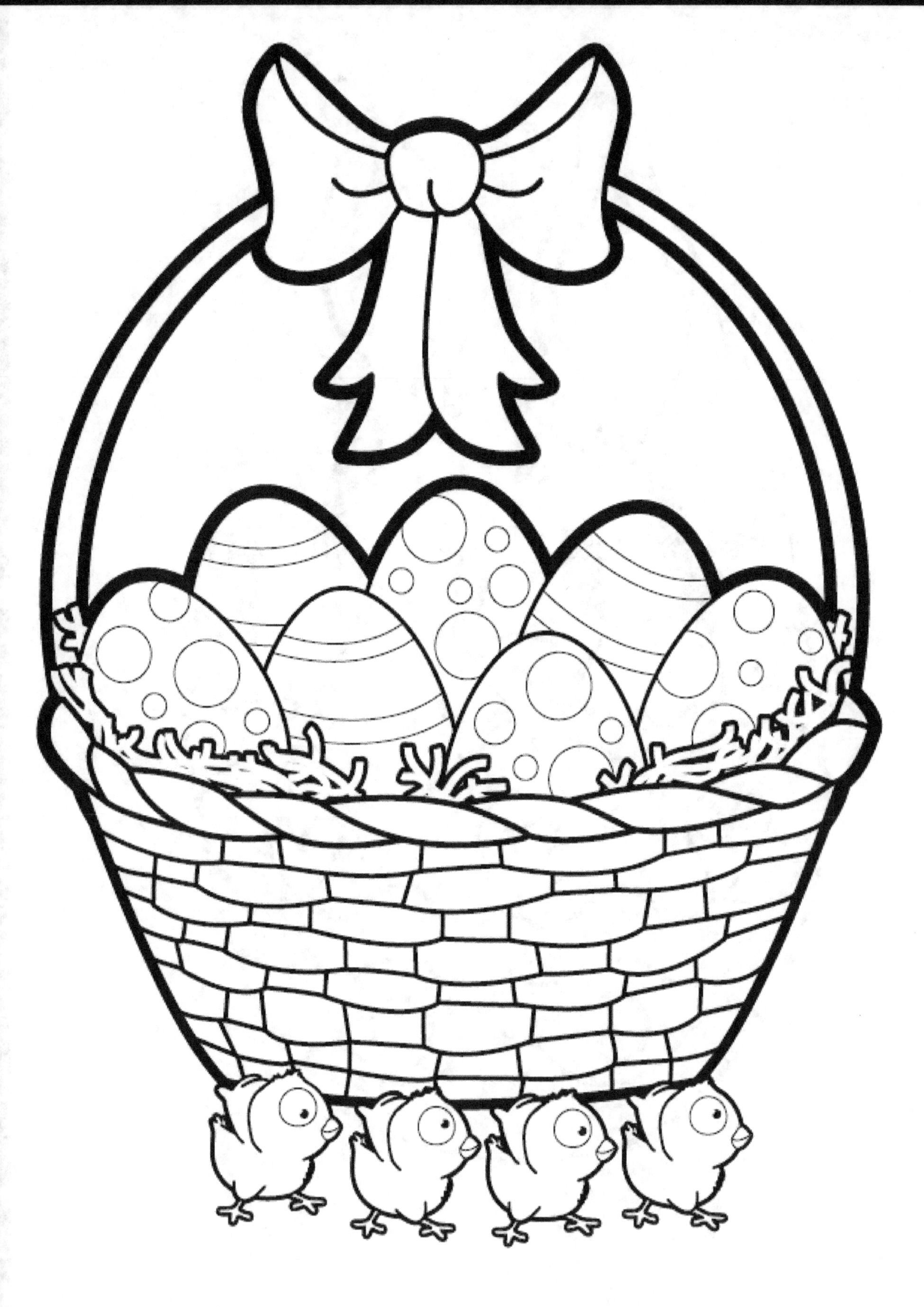

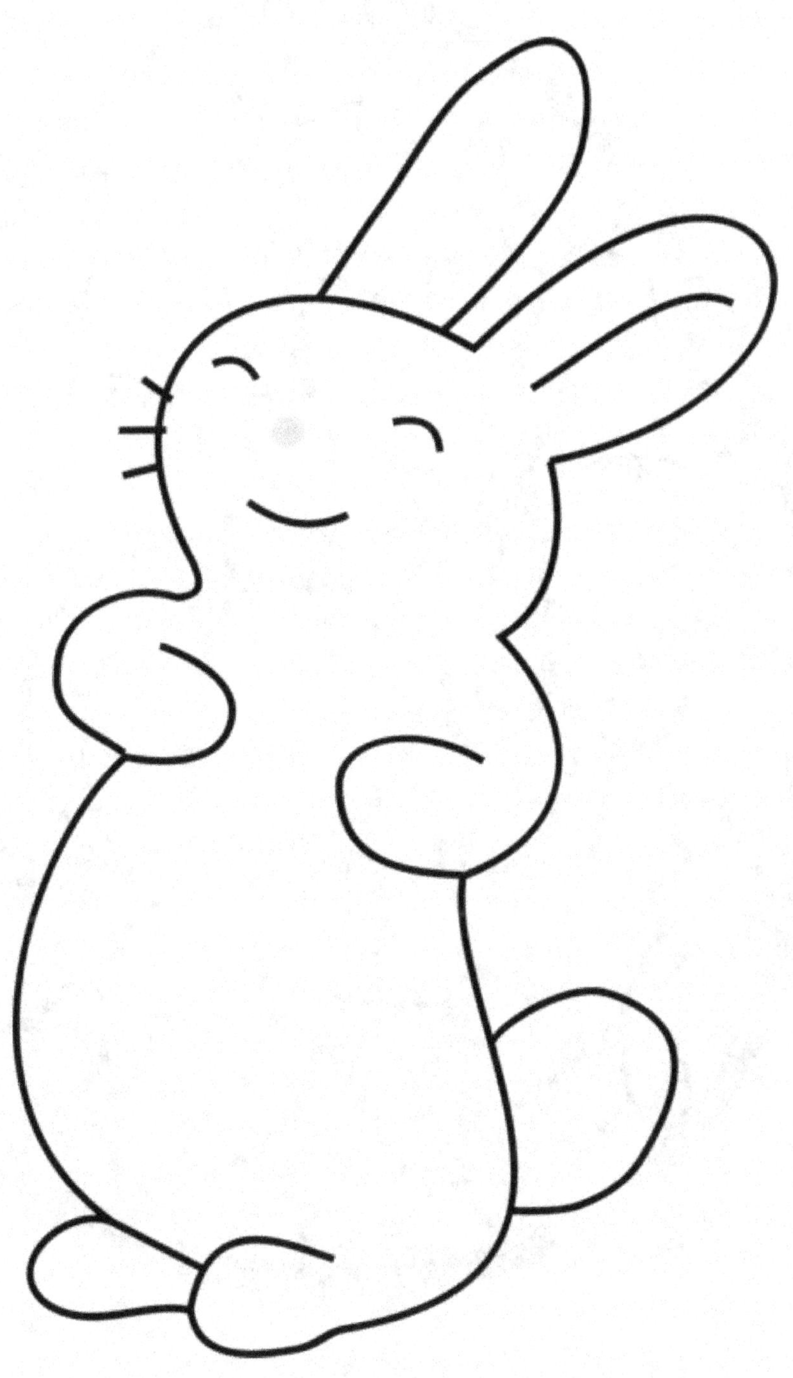

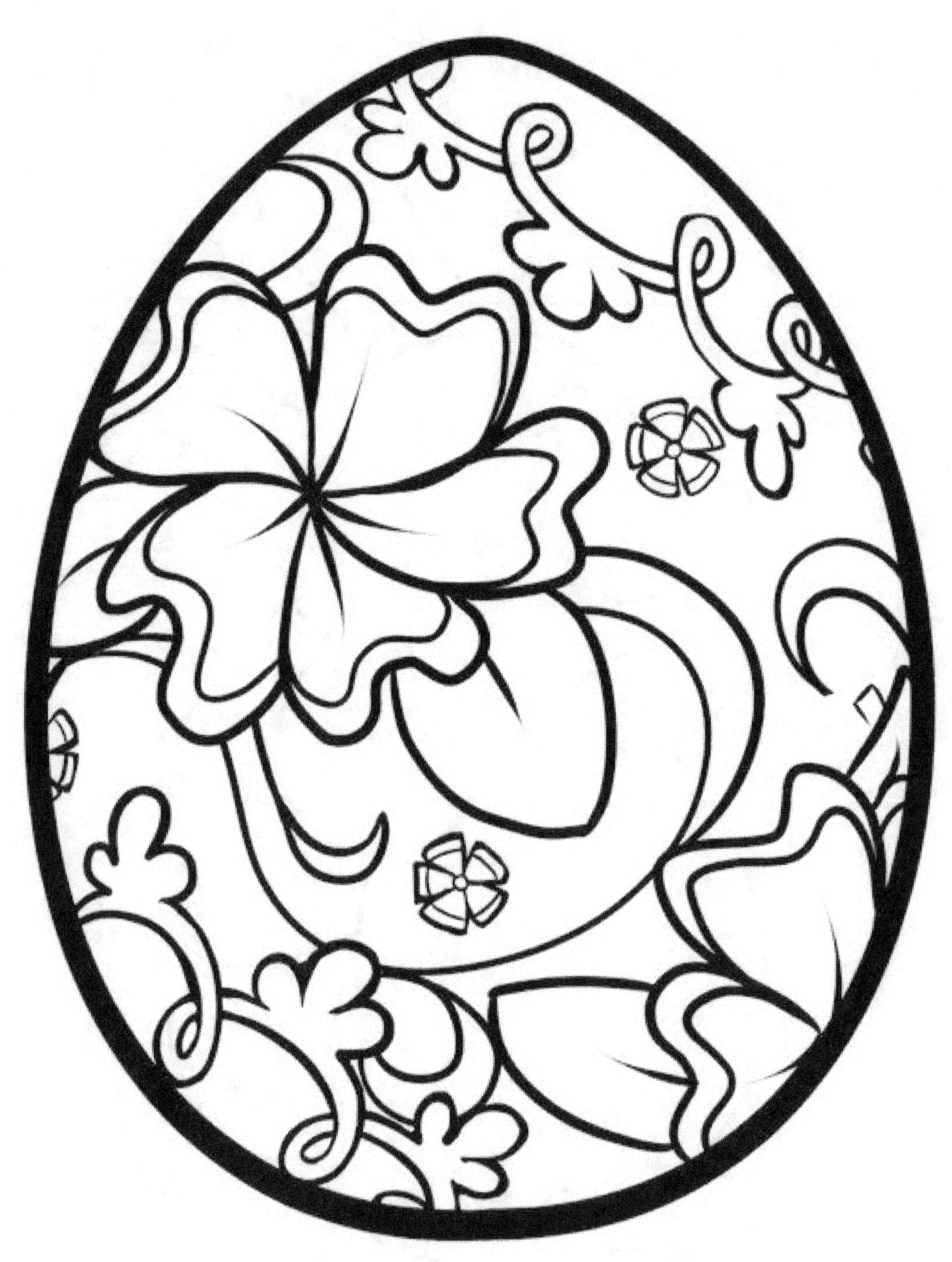

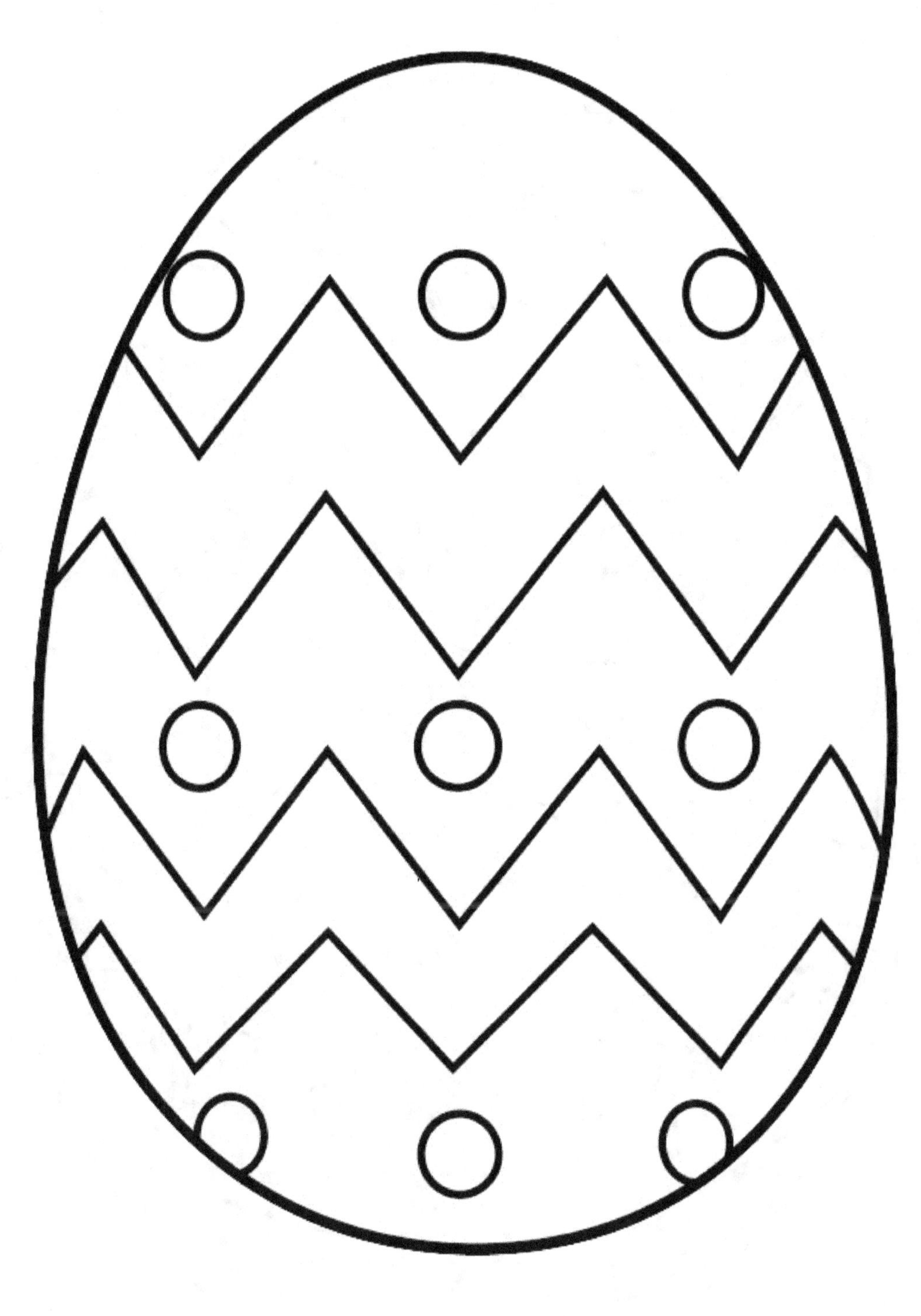

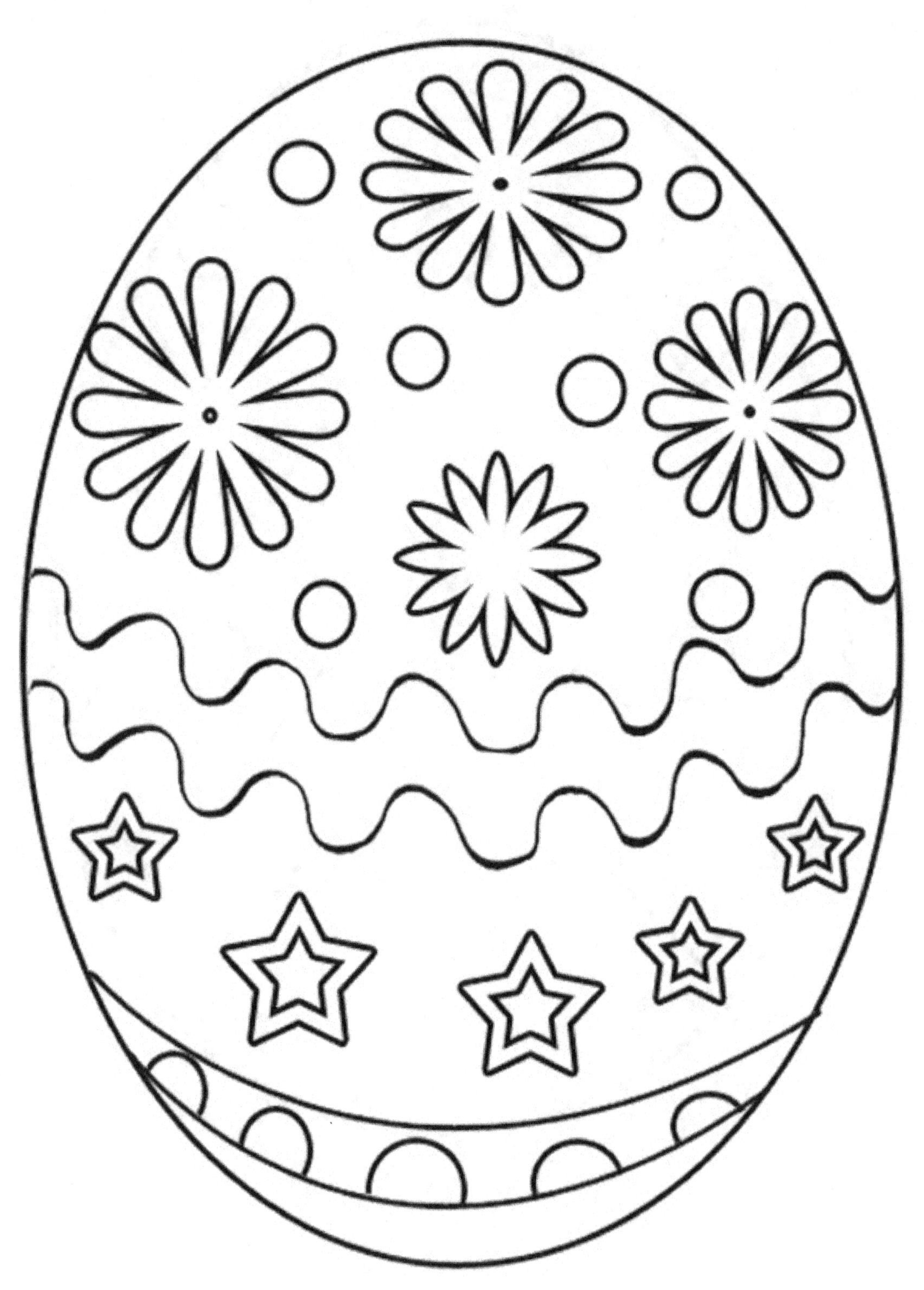

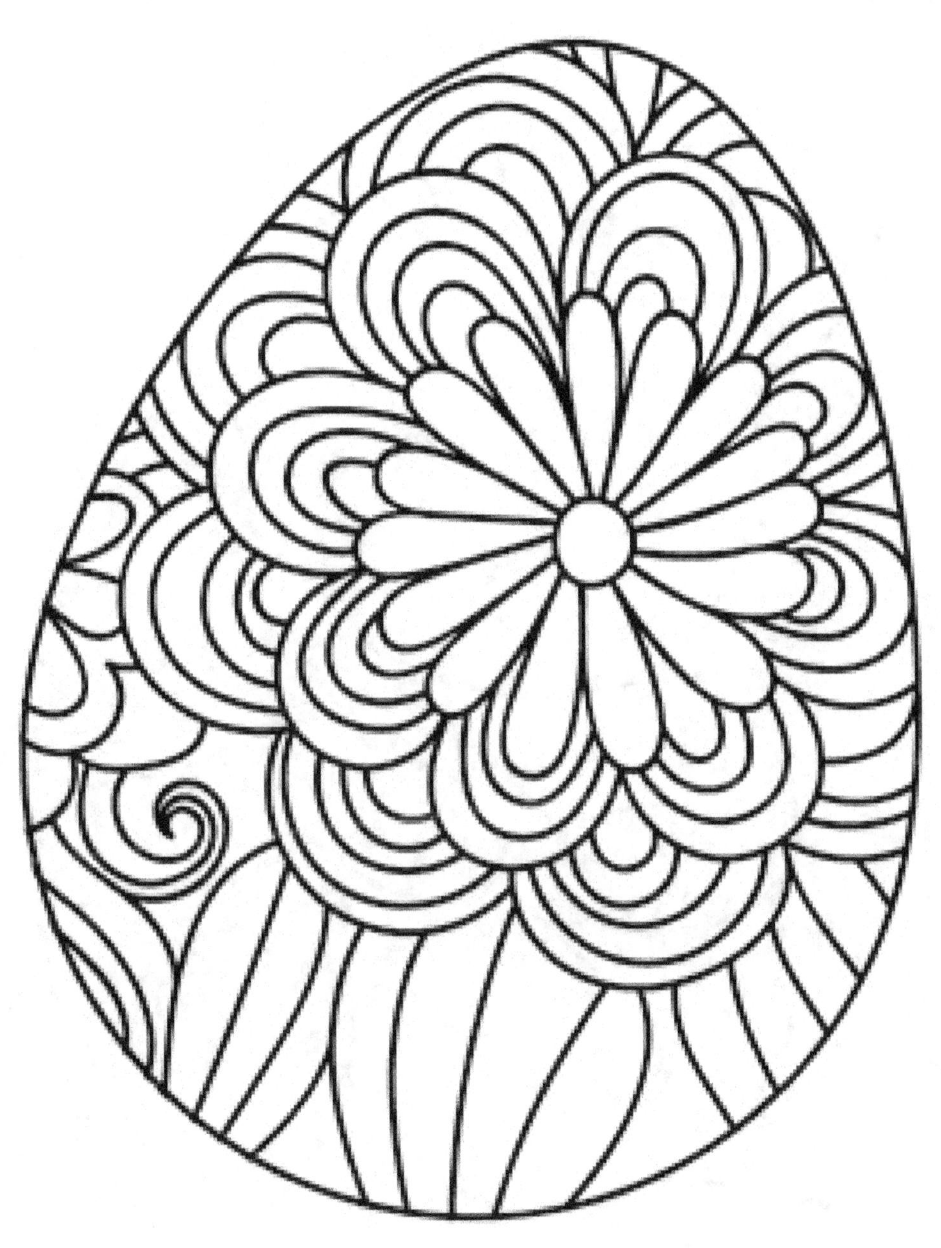

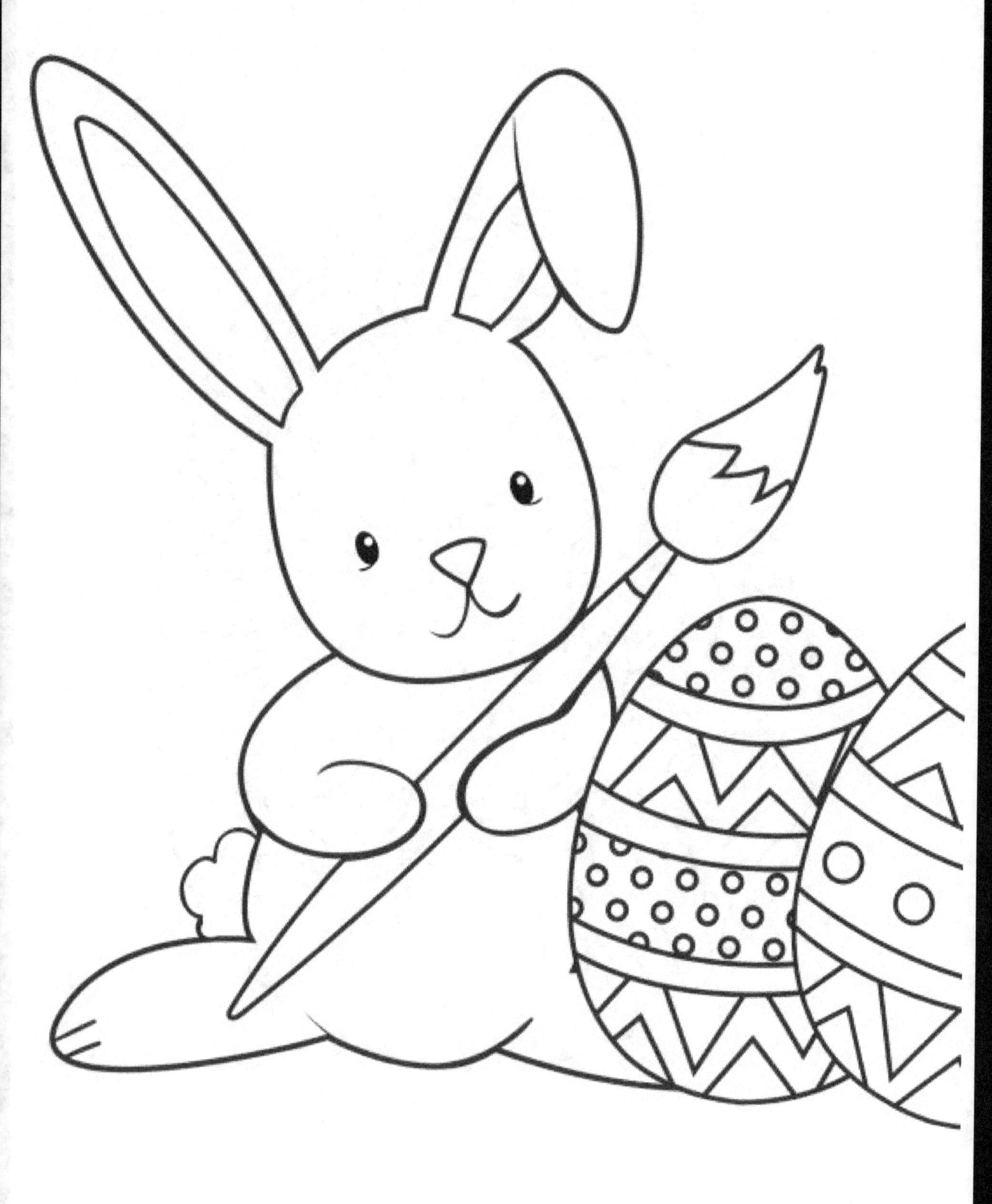

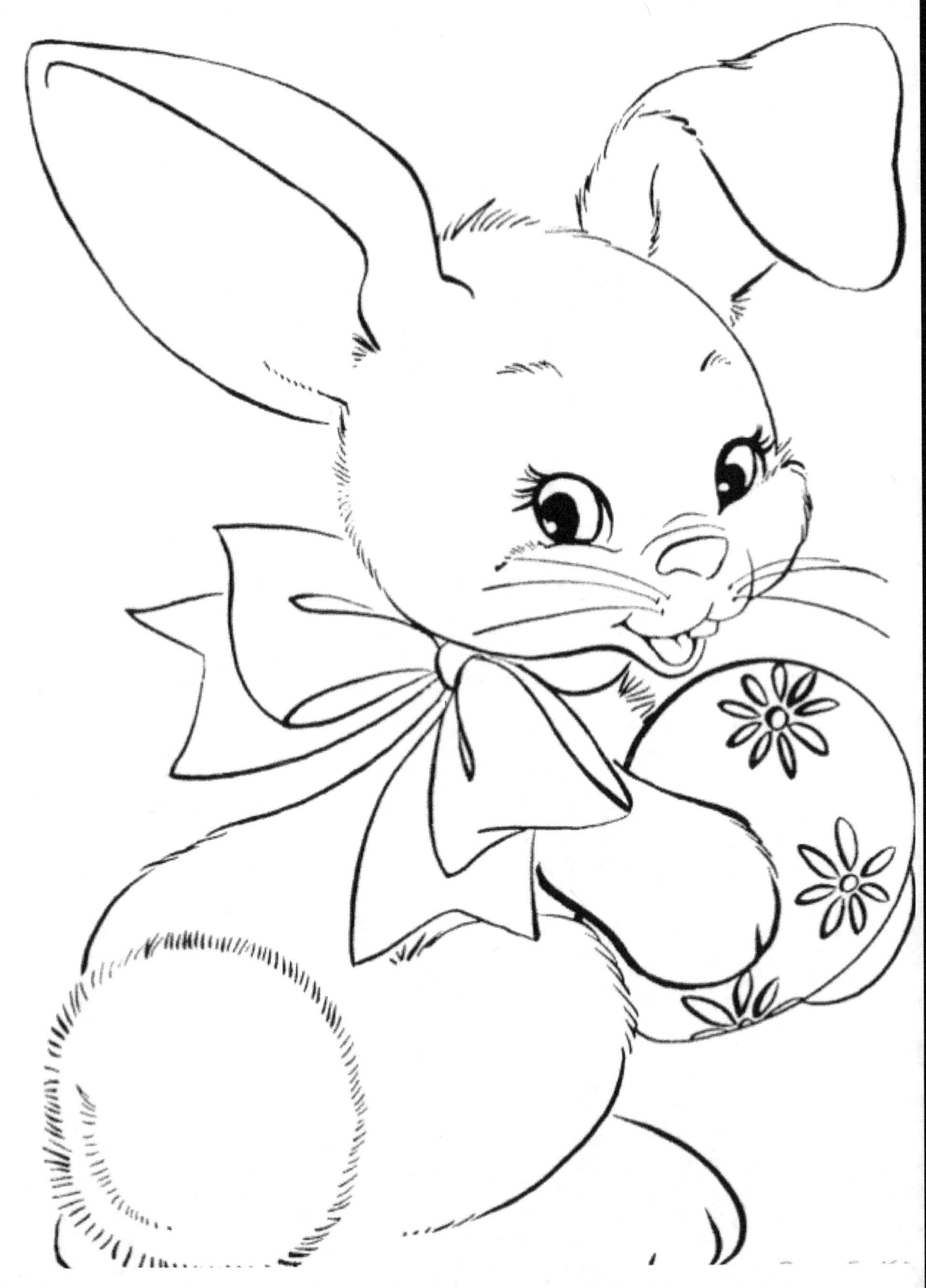

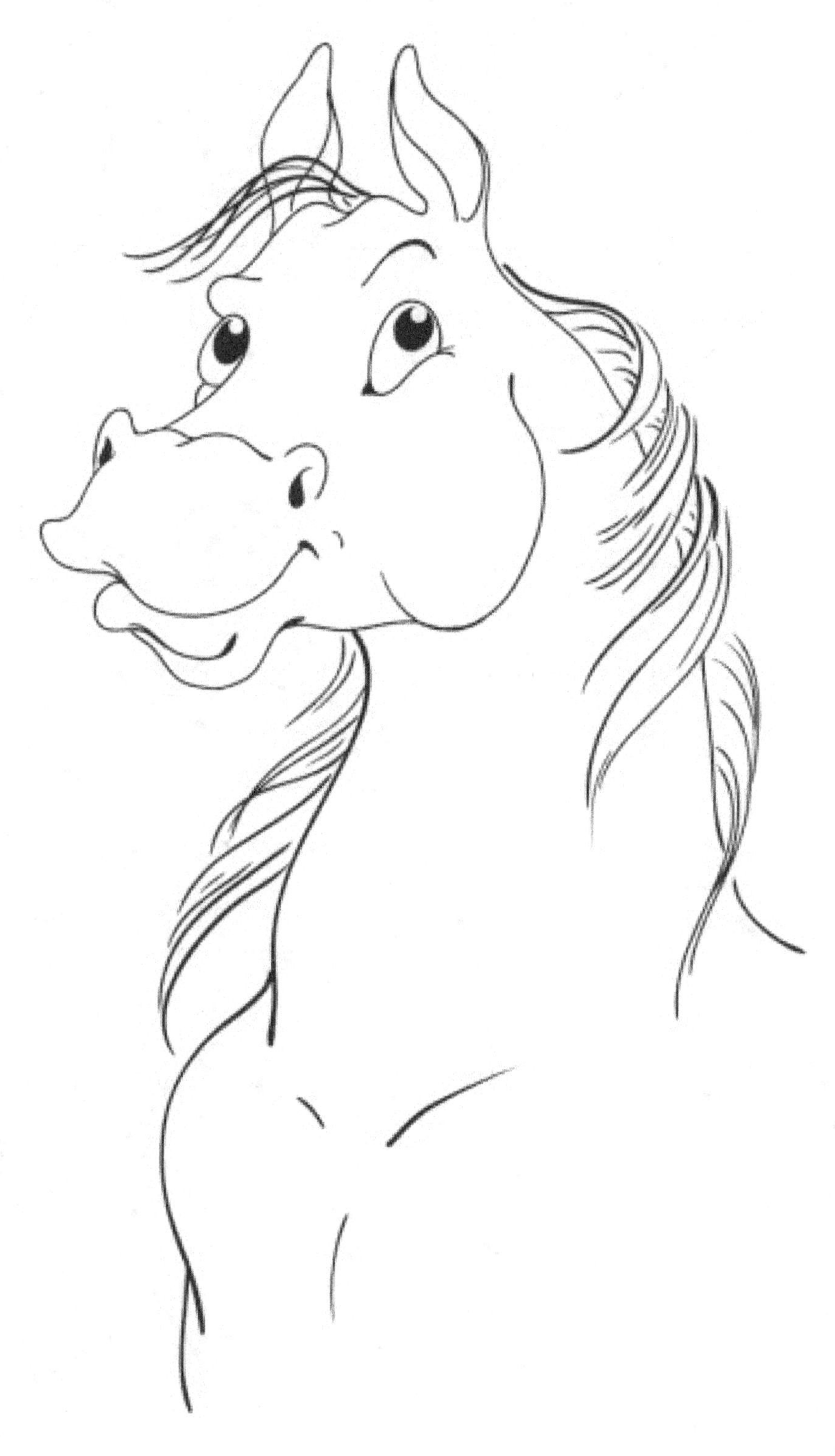

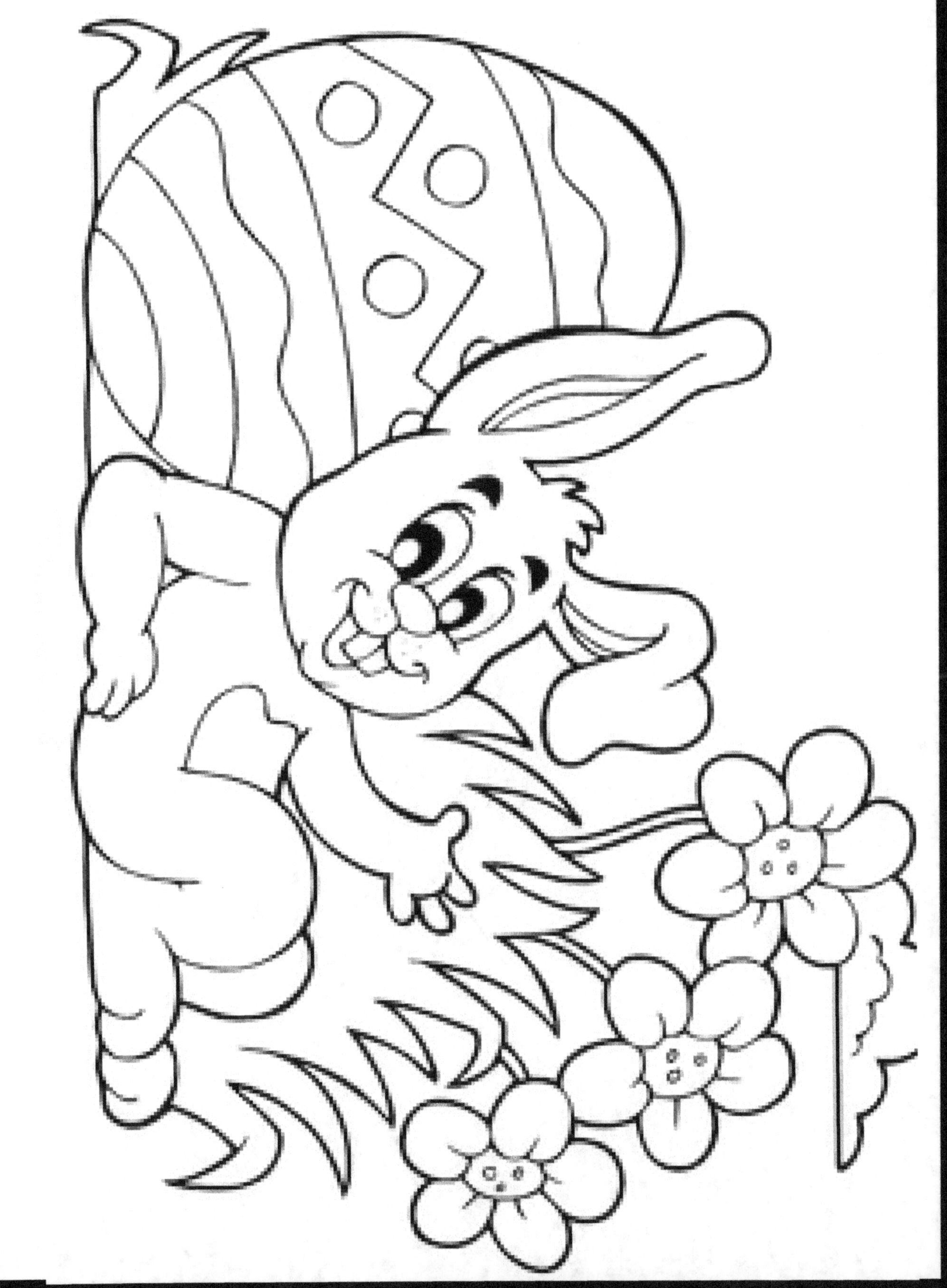

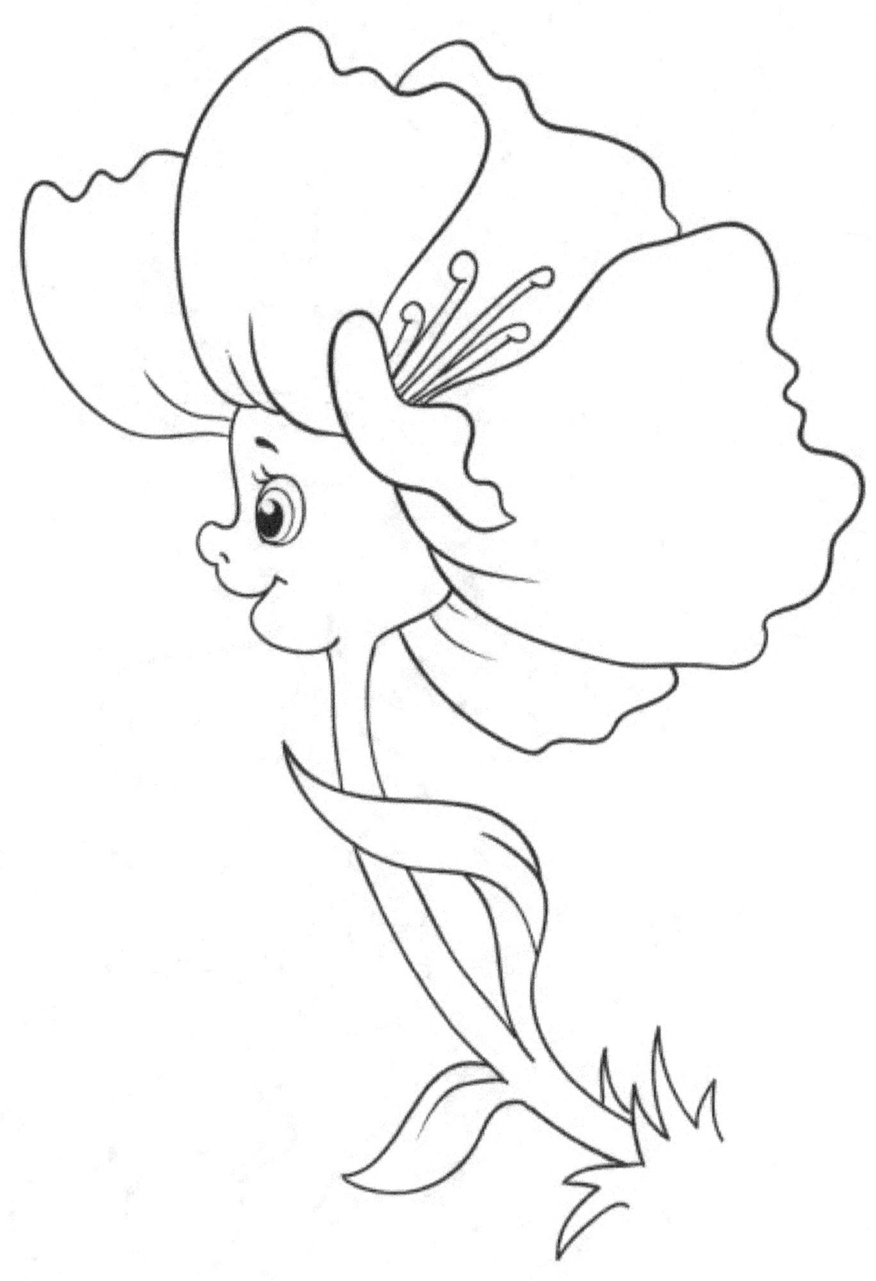

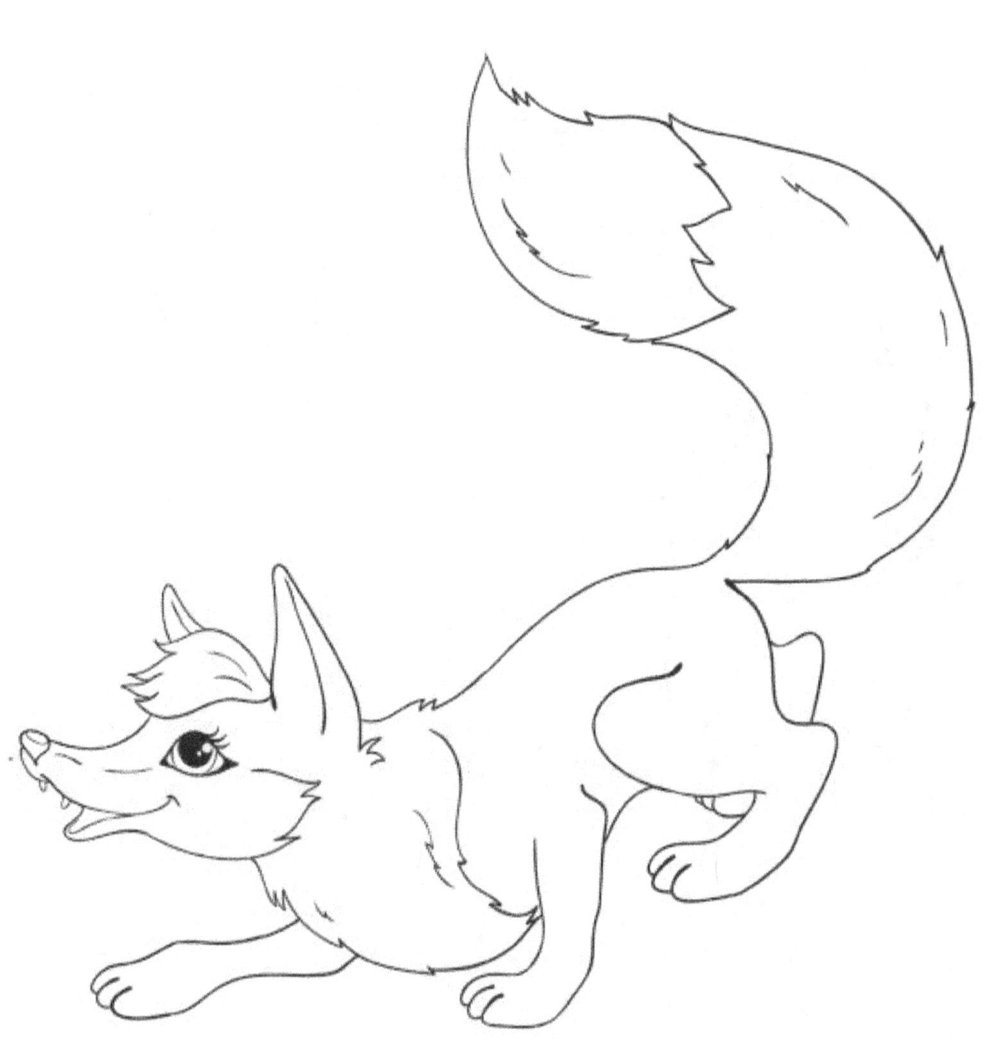

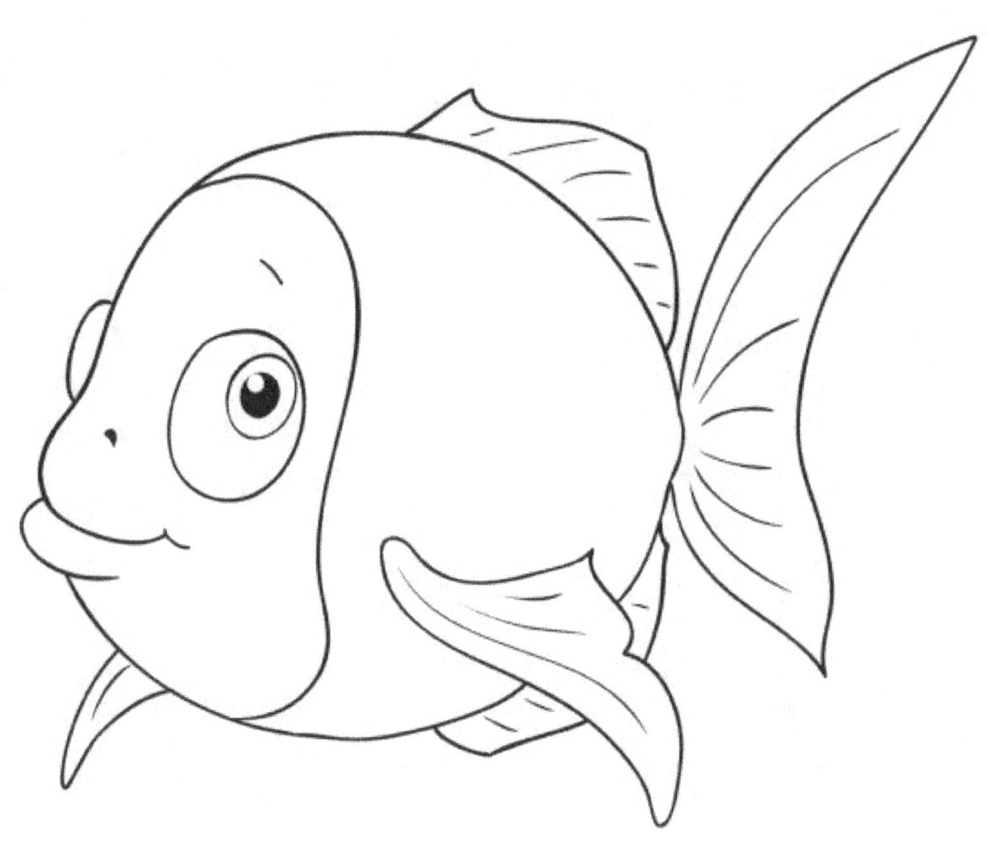

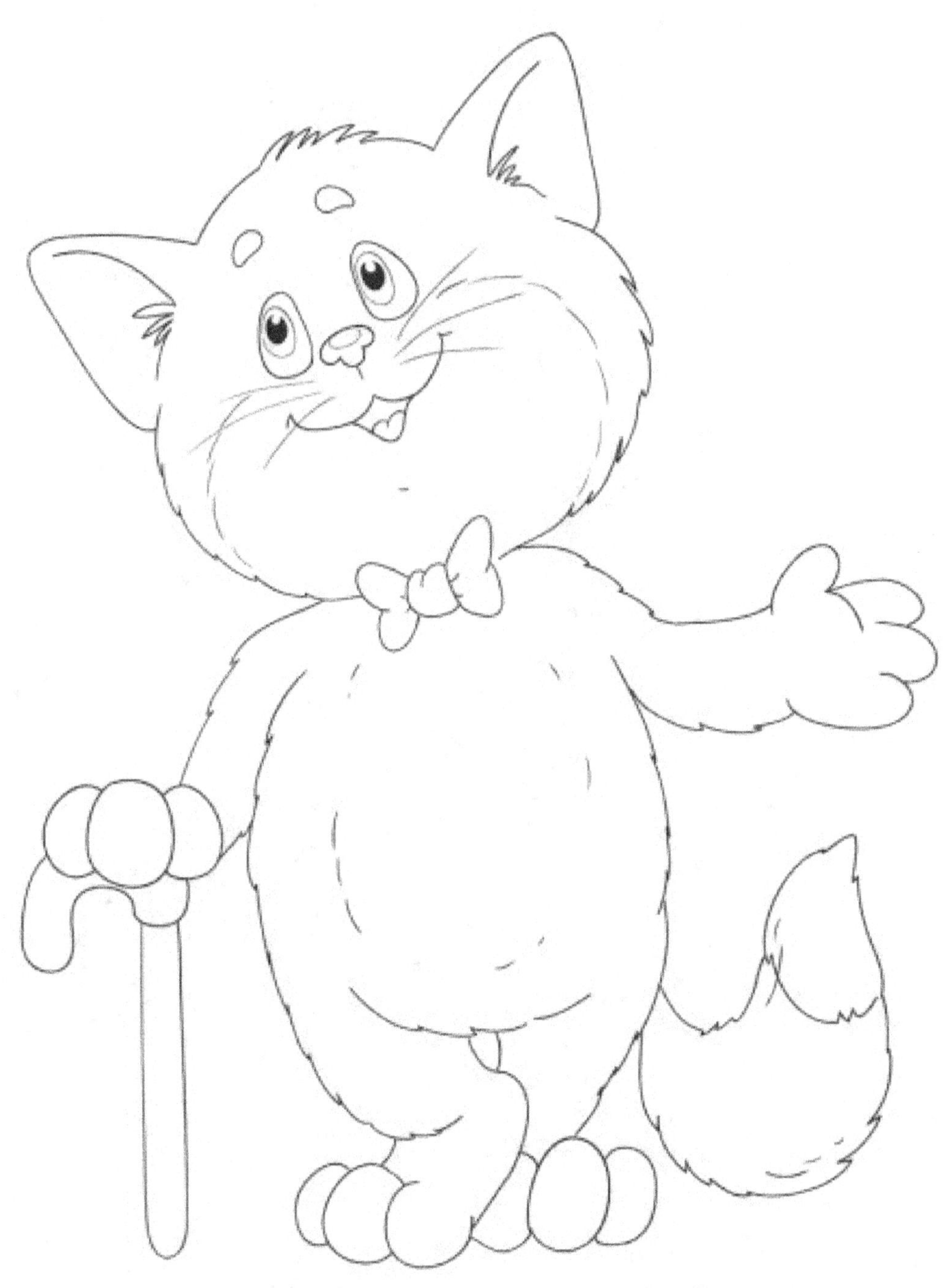

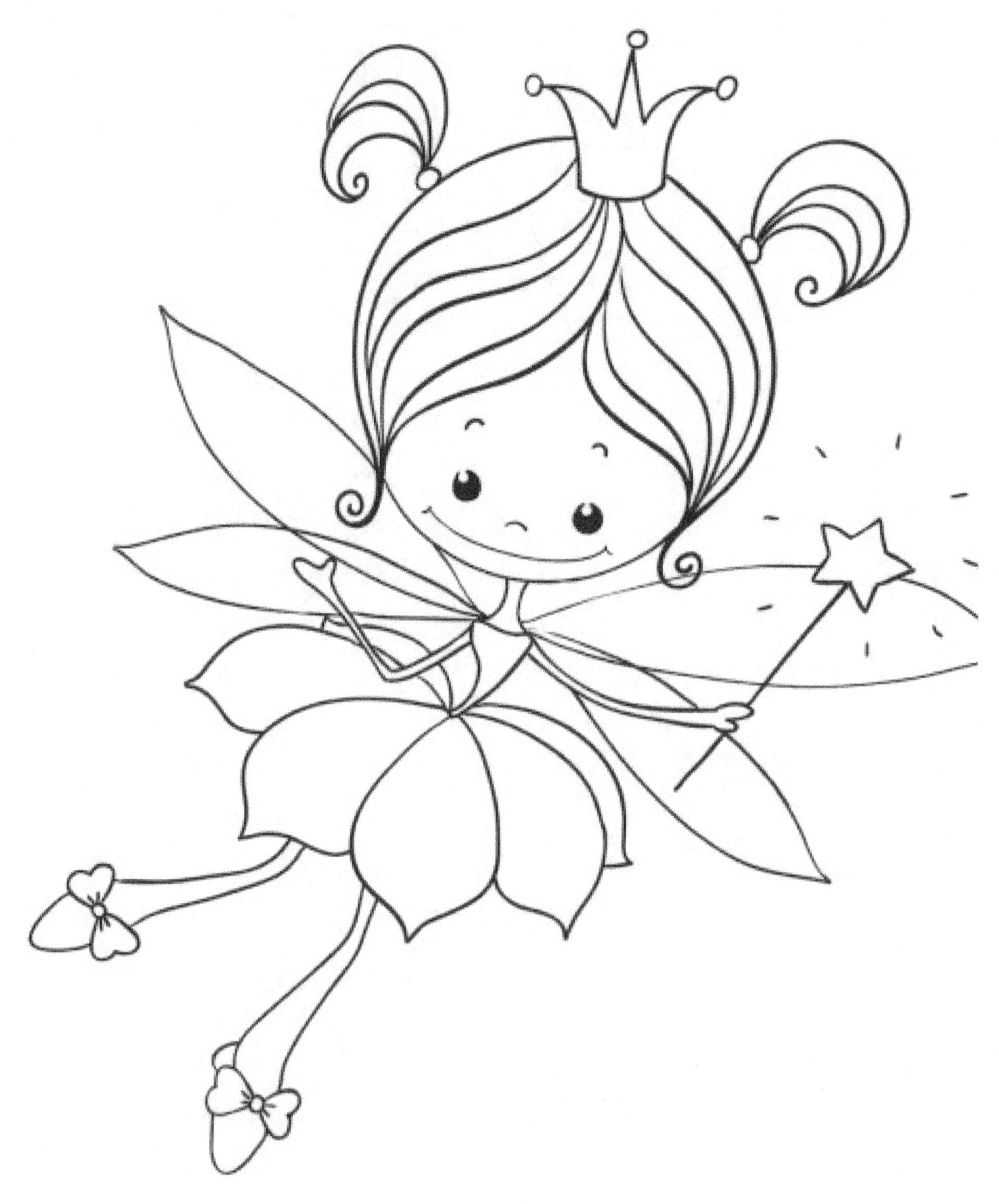

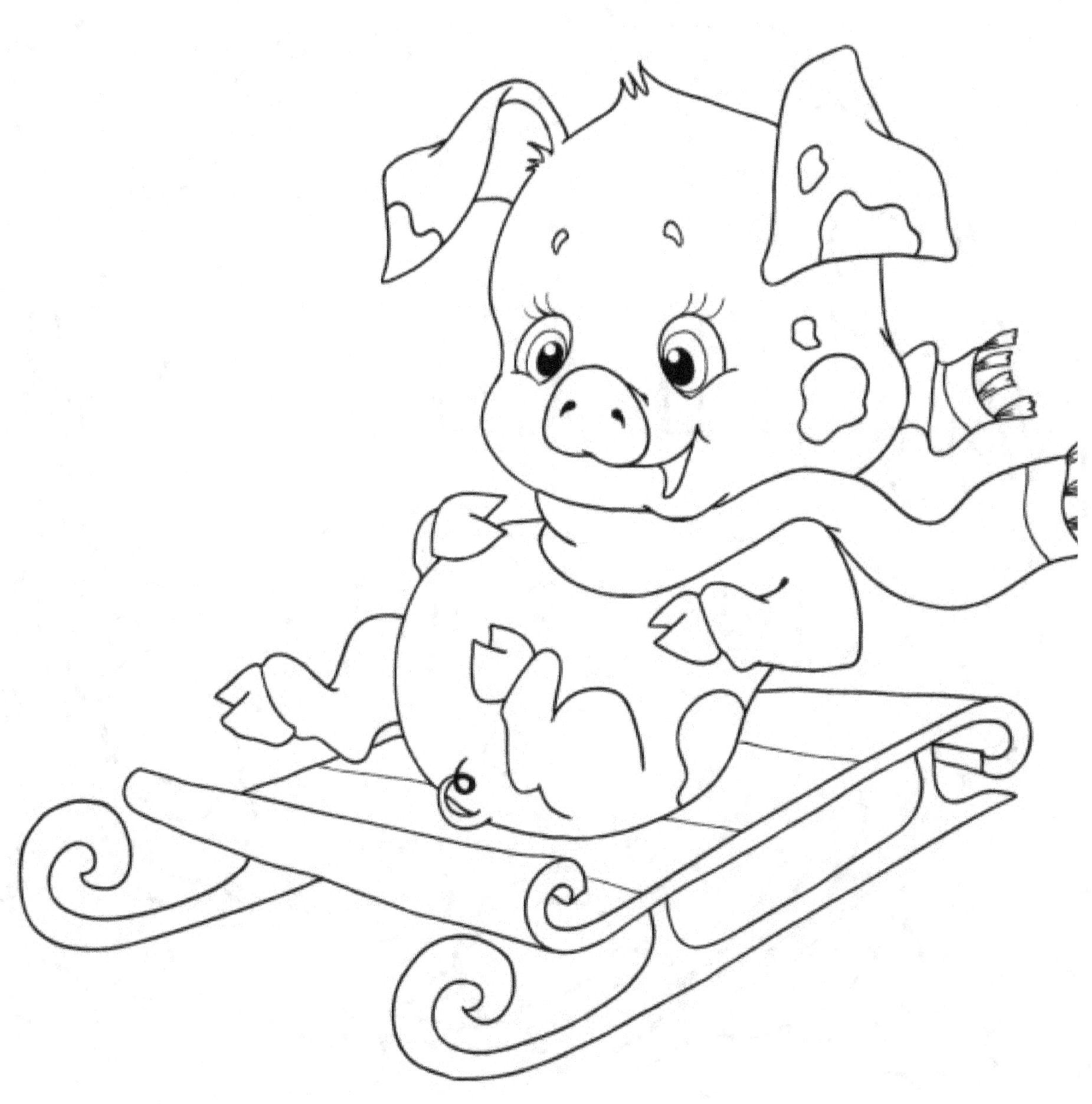

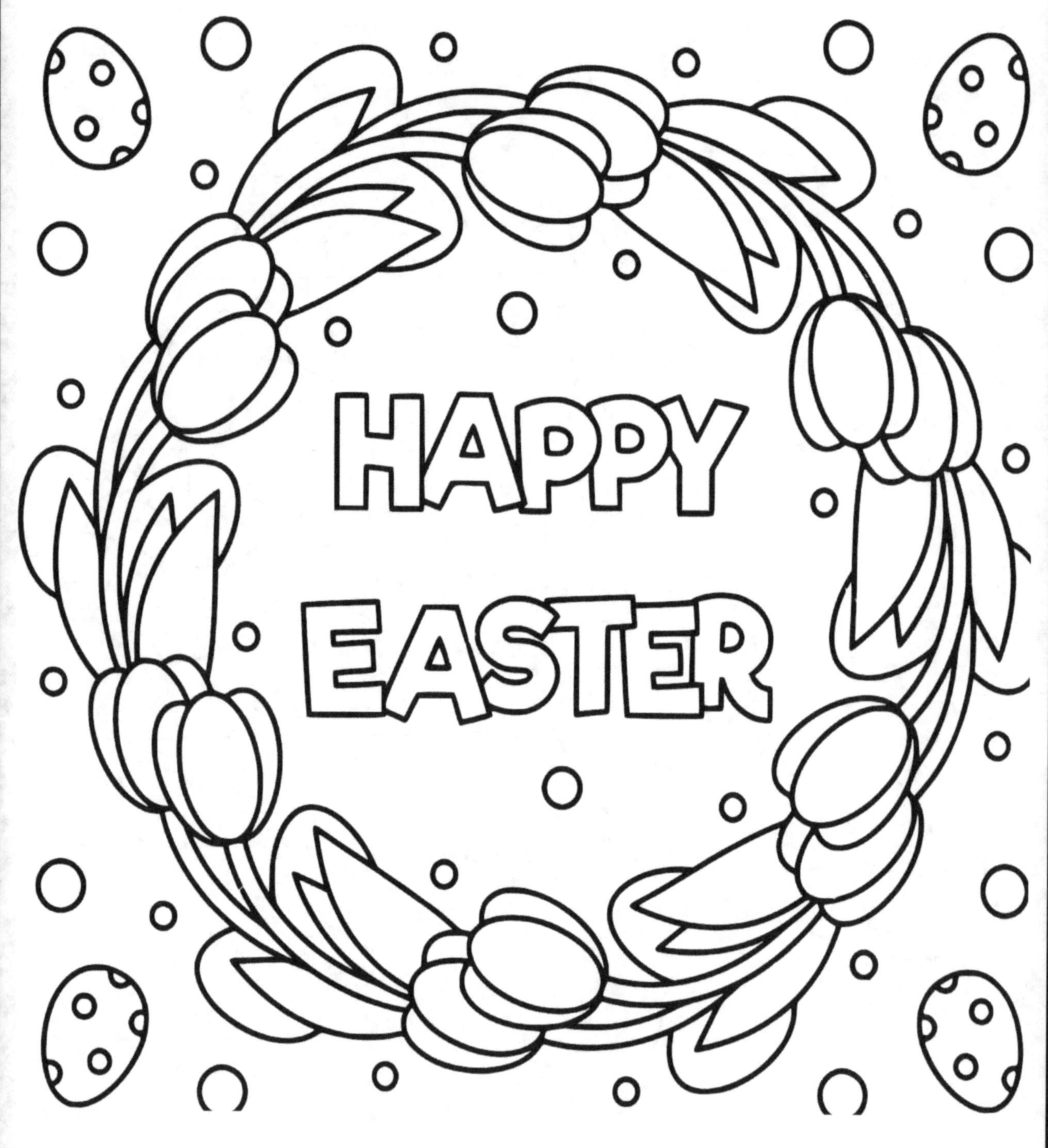
HAPPY
EASTER